TRADITIONAL
SWEDISH
KNITTING PATTERNS

40 motifs and 20 projects

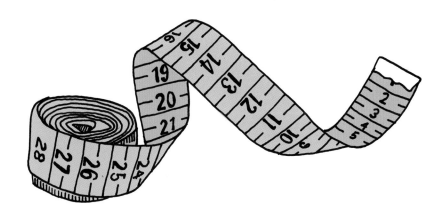

MAJA KARLSSON

TRADITIONAL SWEDISH KNITTING PATTERNS

40 motifs and 20 projects

PHOTOGRAPHY: MARIA ROSENLÖF

TRAFALGAR SQUARE
North Pomfret, Vermont

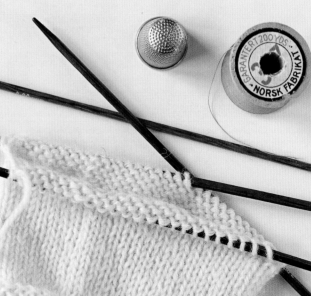

First published in the United States of America
in 2017 by
Trafalgar Square Books
North Pomfret, Vermont 05053

Originally published in Swedish as *Sticka svenska
mönster*.

Copyright © 2016 Bonnier Fakta
English translation © 2017 Trafalgar Square Books

ISBN: 978-1-57076-821-7

Library of Congress Control Number: 2017939362

Pattern instructions and text: Maja Karlsson
Photography: Maria Rosenlöf
Interior graphics: Katy Kimbell
Editor: Annika Ström
Translator: Carol Huebscher Rhoades

Printed in China

10 9 8 7 6 5 4 3 2 1

To my daughter Greta
In memory of my grandmother Greta

CONTENTS

PREFACE

Grandmother's dresser had many drawers—more than I could count. Some of them were impossible for me to reach, even when I stood on tiptoes, but every one of them was filled with treasures. Buttons, sequins, sampler books, photo albums, and knitting needles. Everything was in its place. It always seemed so ceremonial when Grandmother pulled out a drawer and picked out a thing or two. It was just like Christmas Eve.

Grandmother went to the dresser to get knitting needles on the day she taught me how to knit. I was six years old and it might have been spring. We sat at the dinner table—just where the sun shone in. The yarn was light blue and the needles long, thin, and cool. I don't remember whether I thought knitting was hard—only that I knitted. And what I knitted! A little sweater for my teddy bear. Grandmother was so good at finding something "right" to praise about my uneven little swatches.

I was happy with what I'd achieved but I also had a feeling that my bumpy garter stitch looked childish in comparison with Grandmother's perfect stockinette.

"When I'm big," I thought, "then I'll knit as well as Grandmother."

I often think about that day and remember what a gift I was given. Both the ability to knit and the incentive to develop it further. Who would I have become without that gift? For me, the thought makes my mind reel!

At that time, I didn't know how important knitting would be to me: how I would knit through the school years, life's sorrows, vacations at the cottage, winter evenings, train trips, and family holidays—until knitting became a second language, a part of my life, and then finally became my work.

My fascination with knitting's possibilities will never end! To join stitch to stitch and see how a pattern develops is a form of magic I'll never get tired of. It was so much fun delving deep into Swedish knitting traditions as I worked on this book.

I was overcome by seldom-seen splendor—and went to sleep with my head full of flowers, borders, and landscape motifs. I've worked to flat-out transform old patterns into new designs, and tossed and turned over classic motifs. I've knitted like someone possessed to finish a garment—all-nighters, on the train, and at the dinner table... Yes, it pretty much took over everything. I lived with knitting night and day and always with these lovely Swedish patterns close to my heart.

Just think, the starting point for all this was my grandmother Greta teaching me how to knit when I was little. Isn't that amazing?

We never forget the person who taught us how to knit. Ask someone near you and you'll see! Knowledge that migrates from one hand to another invisibly creates a bond that joins us together forever more. In that way, we share in a larger connection and are links in a chain that carries us all further through history. That's what's so wonderful about knitting—it is, quite simply, eternal.

Now it's time for me to send my text and instructions to the publisher. It feels about the same as binding off a sweater. I weave in the ends, take care of the little details, and hope that the book will warm you, the reader. I'm a little nervous, of course—but it's also a lovely feeling! Because even when the binding off is finished, at the same time it's a beginning. Every knitter knows this. Before you can blink, you have cast on something new. What it will become is a story for another time...

Until then—warm knitting wishes from me!

Maja Karlsson, Arvika, Sweden
March 14, 2016

SWEDISH KNITTING PATTERNS

Knitting came to Sweden in the seventeenth century. The earliest pattern motifs were inspired by other textiles such as weavings and embroidery. It was easy to translate well-known motifs into stitches and produce the pattern either through two-color knitting, through switching between knit and purl stitches, or through lace knitting. A weaving technique could be adapted for a texture pattern on a sweater, a woven band could be transformed to a cuff on a sock, and a cross stitch monogram could be translated into stitches and become a marking for a pair of mittens.

In this book, we'll immerse ourselves in the Swedish two-color pattern tradition. The earliest multi-color patterns were very advanced, because many of them had been adapted from the spectacular decorations in other textile techniques. The garments created were firmly knitted and seldom elastic in the way we expect our knitted garments to be today. At the same time that

knitting was discovered, and as knitters became better at using the technique's vast possibilities, a pattern inventory of the unique characteristics of the stitches developed. A fine example of this is the lice* motif that decorates many Swedish and Norwegian garments. The lice are both decorative and important for garment structure, because they contribute to making floats** on the wrong side, which means a thicker and warmer garment.

The patterns in this book are taken primarily from a pattern treasury of the first half of the twentieth century, but many of these patterns' roots go much further back in time. They have developed through individual knitters' variations and modifications. Some belong to a set of eternal symbols and motifs that the art of textiles has maintained for centuries: stripes, flower vines, stars, and blocks. One could almost say that certain motifs are universal, like, for example, the

eight-petaled rose (see opposite)—a star-like symbol that you can find all over the world.

Many influences have come from outside and left their tracks in our pattern traditions; from the beginning, the art of knitting was imported. One example of external influences is the combination of natural black and natural white in pattern knitting—often in the form of folk motifs such as animals, people, hearts, and stars. This tradition arose in Norway in the 1850s and later spread into the Swedish provinces of Jämtland, Härjedalen, Dalarna, Värmland, and Dalsland.

The patterns in this book were taken from my own collections. Over many years, I sought out and conserved old knitted garments, newspaper clippings, pattern booklets, and handwritten notes from flea markets and antique shops. For the most part, these materials have been considered worthless in our time—not least because knitters often stored their standard and favorite patterns in loose-leaf binders that could all too easily be tossed out at the end of the year.

I've been lucky enough to get my hands on some of these collections, thanks to wise heirs who found me and invited me to take the material. Each pattern notebook is unique—and a gold mine! Do you have a pattern notebook at home? Take care of it to help us to conserve our common cultural heritage.

My pattern collection, which is also the foundation for the pattern library in this book, includes knitting magazines (from the 1940s on), newspaper clippings from old scrapbooks, and notes and loose pattern leaflets from knitters' collections—as well as knitted garments. Thanks to all of these materials, it's possible to share the sources of these patterns in the pattern library.

I hope that my book will give you lots of multicolored inspiration, and that the pattern library will inspire you to develop your own creations. Welcome to a world of stars, reindeer, flowers, and all sorts of imaginative figures—and to a pattern archive that is far too pretty to be allowed to fall into the shadows!

THIS BOOK IS DIVIDED INTO FOUR PARTS:

◇ A photo gallery you can look through at your leisure, and the 22 patterns I've designed, based off our Swedish pattern treasury.

◇ A pattern section where you can find instructions for all the garments in the book.

◇ A pattern library that introduces 40 Swedish multi-color designs from my collections.

◇ A knitting school and sources for the yarns used in the book (some of them are Swedish and might be hard to find, but you can always make substitutions; individual yarn descriptions are included in the patterns). In the knitting school I describe and explain certain moments that happen in the pattern section. You'll also find tips and tricks for doing two-color stranded knitting—both for beginners and for anyone who has previously knitted patterns with several colors, but wants to develop their skills.

---

* Lice = individual stitches that are spread regularly over a surface of a contrasting color. The name is Norwegian and used because the stitches look like small lice.

**Float = the strand that is not immediately in use but instead lies across or "floats" on the wrong side of the knitting.

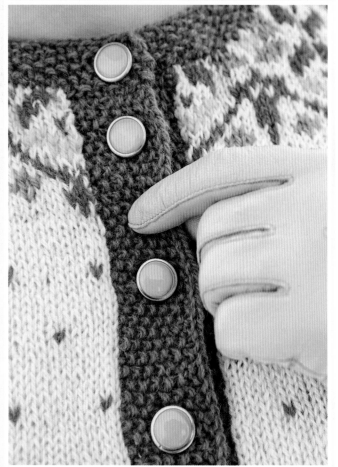

INSTRUCTIONS

A few things to consider regarding the pattern instructions:

◇ Read through the entire pattern before you start to knit, so you have a chance to picture the construction and sequence of production steps.

◇ Always knit a gauge swatch before you start knitting the garment so you can be sure the gauge is correct. Make the swatch about 4¾ x 4¾ in / 12 x 12 cm. Count how many stitches and rows there are in 4 x 4 in / 10 x 10 cm. If your gauge doesn't match the one given in the pattern, adjust the size of the needles. If you have too few stitches per row, try smaller needles; if there are too many stitches per row, try larger needles.

◇ Measurements in the pattern instructions are approximate. Unless otherwise specified, the introductory length, width, and circumference in each pattern are measurements of the garment and not body measurements.

◇ The listed yarn amounts in the instructions are approximate and can differ from knitter to knitter, depending on how loosely or tightly the person knits.

◇ If you don't find the recommended yarn, you can substitute a yarn that has the same fiber content and produces the same gauge.

◇ The amount of light and the season can affect the colors and shades in the photos, so the colors in the pattern photos may look different from the reality.

Rosa
Nostalgic cardigan with rose-pattern panels and puffed sleeves

Rosa is my shout-out to Swedish summer. You'll feel pretty wearing it on a dusky midsummer evening as you follow our tradition: pick seven different flowers to lay under your pillow, and they'll forecast your future love. The rose panel that runs along both front edges can, if you like, be changed out with the band of hearts shown on page 143.

SIZES S (M, L, XL)

FINISHED MEASUREMENTS
Chest: 35½ (39½, 43¼, 47¼) in / 90 (100, 110, 120) cm
Length: 17¾ (17¾, 18¼, 18¼) in / 45 (45, 46, 46) cm
Sleeve length: 16½ (16½, 17, 17) in / 42 (42, 43.5, 43.5) cm

MATERIALS
Yarn: CYCA #3 (DK/light worsted) Hverdagsuld from Tusinfynd (100% wool; 164 yd/150 m / 50 g)

Yarn Amounts:
  MC: 250 (300, 350, 350) g Putty 06
  CC: 50 (50, 50, 50) g Old Rose 18
Needles: U.S. sizes 4 and 6 / 3.5 and 4 mm: 24 in / 60 cm circulars and sets of 5 dpn
Notions: 10 buttons (½–⅝ in / 13–15 mm in diameter); 12 stitch markers
Gauge: 21 sts x 28 rows in St st on larger needles = 4 x 4 in / 10 x 10 cm.
Adjust needle sizes to obtain correct gauge if necessary.

GARMENT CONSTRUCTION AND TECHNIQUES
The sweater is worked from the top down, in one piece.
   Short rows (see Knitting School, page 147) at the back neck are added for a comfortable fit. Increases and decreases on the sleeves produce sweet puffs.
Inc 1 st = increase with a right leaning, M1R, before the raglan marker and with a left-leaning, M1L, after the raglan marker (raglan markers = A, B, C, and D.) For increase techniques, see page 148.
RLI = Right-Lifted Increase (see Knitting School, page 148).

YOKE
With MC and smaller needles, CO 105 sts. Work back and forth in ribbing as follows:
Row 1 (WS): Wyf, sl 1 purlwise, (k1, p1) across.
Row 2 (RS): Wyb, sl 1 knitwise, (p1, k1) across.
Row 3: Work as for Row 1.
Row 4 (buttonhole row): Work as for Row 2 until 4 sts rem, yo, k2tog, p1, k1.
NOTE: Make a buttonhole the same way on every 14th complete row 9 more times.
Row 5: Work as for Row 1.
Row 6: Work as for Row 2.
Row 7: Work as for Row 1, but, *at the same time*, place 4 markers: between sts 22 and 23 (= D), 34 and 35 (= C), 71 and 72 (= B), and 83 and 84 (= A).

The ribbing is now complete. Change to larger needles and work in St st unless otherwise specified.

Row 8 (RS, short row): Work the first 6 sts in ribbing as above and then knit to Marker C; sl m (see Knitting School, page 150), k6, wrap st; turn (see Knitting School, page 147).

Row 9 (WS, short row): Purl to Marker B, sl m, p6, wrap st; turn.

Row 10 (RS, short row): Knit to Marker D, sl m, wrap st; turn.

Row 11 (WS, short row): Purl to Marker A, sl m, wrap st; turn.

Row 12 (RS, short row): Knit until 6 sts rem, work the last 6 sts in ribbing as above.

Row 13: Work the first 6 sts in ribbing as before, purl until 6 sts rem and work the last 6 sts in ribbing.

Now begin the shaping for the raglan yoke and puffed sleeves and set up the rose panels. Don't forget to make the buttonholes!

Row 14: Work 6 sts in ribbing, k2, work following Chart A, adding in CC, knit until 1 st rem before Marker A, M1, k1, sl m, k1, M1, (RLI) 10 times, M1, k1, sl m B, k1, M1, Knit until 1 st rem before Marker C, M1, k1, sl m, k1, M1, (RLI) 10 times, M1, k1, sl m D, k1, M1. Knit until 17 sts rem, work following Chart B with CC, k2, work 6 sts in ribbing = 133 sts.

Row 15:

Size S: Work 6 sts in ribbing, p2, work Chart B, purl until 17 sts rem, work Chart A, p2, 6 sts in ribbing = 133 sts.

Sizes M/L/XL: Work 6 sts in ribbing, p2, work Chart B. Purl until 1 st rem before Marker D, M1, p1, sl m, p1, M1. Purl until 1 st before Marker C, M1, p1, sl m, p1, M1. Purl until 1 st before Marker B, M1, p1, sl m, p1, M1. Purl until 1 st before Marker A, M1, p1, sl m, p1, M1. Purl until 17 sts rem, work Chart A, p2, work 6 sts in ribbing = 141 sts.

Row 16: Work 6 sts in ribbing, k1, work Chart A, knit until 1 st before Marker A, M1, k1, sl m, k1, M1, k0 (1, 1, 1), (RLI) 22 times, k0 (1, 1, 1), M1, k1, sl m B, k1, M1. Knit until 1 sts rem before Marker C, M1, k1, sl m, k1, M1, k0 (1, 1, 1), (RLI) 22 times, k0 (1, 1, 1), M1, k1, sl m D, k1, M1. Knit until 17 sts rem, work Chart B, k2, work 6 sts in ribbing = 185 (193, 193, 193) sts.

Row 17: Work as for Row 15 = 185 (201, 201, 201) sts.

Row 18: Work 6 sts in ribbing, k1, work Chart A, knit until 1 st before Marker A, M1, k1, sl m, k1, M1. Knit until 1 st before Marker B, M1, k1, sl m, k1, M1. Knit until 1 st rem before Marker C, M1, k1, sl m, k1, M1. Knit until 1 st before Marker D, k1, M1, sl m, k1, M1. Knit until 17 sts rem, work Chart B, k2, work 6 sts in ribbing = 193 (209, 209, 209) sts.

Row 19:

Sizes S/M: Work 6 sts in ribbing, p2, work Chart B, purl until 17 sts rem, work Chart A, p2, 6 sts in ribbing = 193 (209) sts.

Sizes L/XL: Work 6 sts in ribbing, p2, work Chart B. Purl until 1 st rem before Marker D, M1, p1, sl m, p1, M1. Purl until 1 st before Marker C, M1, p1, sl m, p1, M1. Purl until 1 st before Marker B, M1, p1, sl m, p1, M1. Purl until 1 st before Marker A, M1, p1, sl m, p1, M1. Purl until 17 sts rem, work Chart A, p2, work 6 sts in ribbing = 217 (217) sts.

Row 20: Work as for Row 18 = 201 (217, 225, 225) sts.

Row 21: Work as for Row 19 = 201 (217, 233, 233) sts.

Row 22: Work as for Row 18 = 209 (225, 241, 241) sts.

Row 23: Work as for Row 19 = 209 (225, 249, 249) sts.

Row 24: Work as for Row 18 = 217 (233, 257, 257) sts.

Row 25:

Sizes S/M/L: Work 6 sts in ribbing, p2, work Chart B, purl until 17 sts rem, work Chart A, p2, 6 sts in ribbing = 217 (233, 257) sts.

Size XL: Work 6 sts in ribbing, p2, work Chart B. Purl until 1 st rem before Marker D, M1, p1, sl m, p1, M1.

Purl until 1 st before Marker C, M1, p1, sl m, p1, M1. Purl until 1 st before Marker B, M1, p1, sl m, p1, M1. Purl until 1 st before Marker A, M1, p1, sl m, p1, M1. Purl until 17 sts rem, work Chart A, p2, work 6 sts in ribbing = 265 sts.

Row 26: Work as for Row 18 = 225 (241, 265, 273) sts.

Row 27:

Sizes S/M/L: Work 6 sts in ribbing, p2, work Chart B, purl until 17 sts rem, work Chart A, p2, 6 sts in ribbing.

Size XL: Work 6 sts in ribbing, p2, work Chart B. Purl until 1 st rem before Marker D, M1, p1, sl m, p1, M1. Purl until 1 st before Marker C, M1, p1, sl m, p1, M1. Purl until 1 st before Marker B, M1, p1, sl m, p1, M1. Purl until 1 st before Marker A, M1, p1, sl m, p1, M1. Purl until 17 sts rem, work Chart A, p2, work 6 sts in ribbing = 281 sts.

Row 28: Work as for Row 18 = 233 (249, 273, 289) sts.

Row 29: Work as for Row 27 *but do not increase for size XL* = 233 (249, 273, 289) sts.

Row 30: Work as for Row 18 = 241 (257, 281, 297) sts.

Row 31: Work 6 sts in ribbing, p2, work Chart B, purl until 17 sts rem, work Chart A, p2, 6 sts in ribbing.

Row 32: Work as for Row 18 = 249 (265, 289, 305) sts.

Row 33: Work as for Row 31, but, *at the same time*, place 8 markers on puffed sleeves.

Size S: Count out from Marker D and place markers between sts 12 and 13, 23 and 24, 41 and 42, 52 and 53. Place markers correspondingly counted out from Marker B.

Size M: Count out from Marker D and place markers between sts 14 and 15, 25 and 26, 43 and 44, 54 and 55. Place markers correspondingly counted out from Marker B.

Size L: Count out from Marker D and place markers between sts 17 and 18, 28 and 29, 46 and 47, 57 and 58. Place markers correspondingly counted out from Marker B.

Size XL: Count out from Marker D and place markers between sts 20 and 21, 31 and 32, 49 and 50, 60 and 61. Place markers correspondingly counted out from Marker B.

NOTE: The raglan increases continue *at the same time* as the puffed sleeves begin decreasing.

Row 34: Work 6 sts in ribbing, k1, work Chart A, knit until 1 st before Marker A, M1, k1, sl m, k1, M1. (Knit to puffed sleeve marker, sl m, ssk) 2 times. (Knit until 2 sts before puffed sleeve marker, k2tog, sl m) 2 times. Knit until 1 st before Marker B, M1, k1, sl m, k1, M1. Knit until 1 st before Marker C, M1, k1, sl m, k1, M1. (Knit

to next puffed sleeve marker, sl m, ssk) 2 times. (Knit until 2 sts before puffed sleeve marker, k2tog, sl m) 2 times. Knit until 1 st before Marker D, M1, k1, sl m, k1, M1. Knit until 17 sts rem, work Chart B, k2, work 6 sts in ribbing.

Row 35: Work 6 sts in ribbing, p2, work Chart B, purl until 17 sts rem, work Chart A, p2, work 6 sts in ribbing.

Rows 36–45: Rep Rows 34 and 35.

Row 46: Work as for Row 34.

Row 47: Work as for Row 35 = 249 (265, 289, 305) sts rem.

The 7 decrease rows for the puffed sleeves are now complete and you can remove the puffed sleeves markers.

Row 48: Work as for Row 18 = 257 (273, 297, 313) sts.

Row 49: Work 6 sts in ribbing, p2, work Chart B, purl until 17 sts rem, work Chart A, p2, work 6 sts in ribbing.

Row 50: Work as for Row 18 = 265 (281, 305, 321) sts.

Row 51: Work 6 sts in ribbing, p2, work Chart B, purl until 17 sts rem, work Chart A, p2, work 6 sts in ribbing.

Row 52: Work as for Row 18 = 273 (289, 313, 329) sts.

Row 53: Work 6 sts in ribbing, p2, work Chart B, purl until 17 sts rem, work Chart A, p2, work 6 sts in ribbing.

The raglan increases for size XL are now complete. There have been a total of 27 increase rows = 329 sts.

SIZES S/M/L ONLY

Row 54: Work as for Row 18.

Row 55: Work 6 sts in ribbing, p2, work Chart B, purl until 17 sts rem, work Chart A, p2, work 6 sts in ribbing.

The raglan increases for size L are now complete. There have been a total of 26 increase rows = 321 sts.

SIZES S/M ONLY

Row 56: Work as for Row 18.

Row 57: Work 6 sts in ribbing, p2, work Chart B, purl until 17 sts rem, work Chart A, p2, work 6 sts in ribbing.

Row 58: Work as for Row 18.

Row 59: Work 6 sts in ribbing, p2, work Chart B, purl until 17 sts rem, work Chart A, p2, work 6 sts in ribbing.

The raglan increases for size M are now complete. There have been a total of 25 increase rows = 313 sts.

SIZE S ONLY

Row 60: Work as for Row 18.

Row 61: Work 6 sts in ribbing, p2, work Chart B, purl until 17 sts rem, work Chart A, p2, work 6 sts in ribbing.

The raglan increases for size S are now complete. There have been a total of 24 increase rows = 305 sts.

Continue to increase for the body by repeating Rows 1-2 below a total of 4 (7, 10, 13) times.

Row 1: Work 6 sts in ribbing, k1, work Chart A, knit until 1 st rem before Marker A, M1, k1, sl m. Knit to Marker B, sl m, k1, M1. Knit until 1 st before Marker C, M1, k1, sl m. Knit to Marker D, sl m, k1, M1. Knit until 17 sts rem, work Chart B, k2, work 6 sts in ribbing.

Row 2: Work 6 sts in ribbing, p2, work Chart B, purl until 17 sts rem, work Chart A, p2, work 6 sts in ribbing.

There are now 321 (341, 361, 381) sts total.

DIVIDE FOR BODY AND SLEEVES

Row 1: Work 50 (54, 58, 62) sts as est with ribbing and rose panel (= right front); sl m (which is now a side marker), place 64 (66, 68, 70) sts on a holder (= right sleeve). Remove marker, work 93 (101, 109, 117) sts (= back), sl m (which now becomes a side marker). Place 64 (66, 68, 70) sts on a holder (= left sleeve); remove marker. Work 50 (54, 58, 62) sts as est with rose panel and ribbing (= left front) = 193 (209, 225, 241) sts rem.

Row 2: Work 6 sts in ribbing, p2, work Chart B, purl until 17 sts rem, work Chart A, p2, work 6 sts in ribbing.

BODY

Row 1: Work 6 sts in ribbing, k2, work Chart A, knit until 17 sts rem, work Chart B, k2, 6 sts in ribbing.

Row 2: Work 6 sts in ribbing, p2, work Chart B, purl until 17 sts rem, work Chart A, p2, work 6 sts in ribbing

Rep Rows 1–2 until piece measures ¾ in / 2 cm from division into sections. End with a WS row.

Now shape the body with decreases at the sides. Work decreases on RS rows as follows:

Work 6 sts in ribbing, k2, work Chart A, *knit until 3 sts rem before the first side marker, ssk, k1, sl m, k1, k2tog*. Rep from * to * once more, knit until 17 sts rem, work Chart B, k2, work 6 sts in ribbing (= 4 sts decreased).

Continue working as est with the ribbed edge and rose panels, repeating the decrease row every 6th row 0 (0, 1, 2) times, every 8th row 3 (4, 3, 2) times, and then every 10th row 1 (0, 0, 0) times = 173 (189, 205, 221) sts rem.

Continue without further shaping, maintaining the ribbing and rose panels until there are 5 roses total. Continue until piece measures 6¾ (6¾, 7, 7) in / 17 (17, 18, 18) cm from division. End with a WS row.

Change to smaller needles and work in k1, p1 ribbing, slipping the first st of each row as before for 2½ in / 6 cm. End with a WS row and then BO in ribbing.

SLEEVES

Divide the 64 (66, 68, 70) sleeve sts onto larger size dpn, as evenly as possible. Attach MC and pick up and knit 1 st at underarm, k64 (66, 68, 70), pick up and knit 1 st at underarm; pm for beg of rnd = 66 (68, 70, 72) sts. Knit 32 (32, 37 37) rnds.

Begin sleeve shaping:

Decrease Rnd: K1, ssk, knit until 3 sts rem before marker, k2tog, k1 (= 2 sts decreased).

Rep the decrease rnd every 8th rnd 9 more times = 46 (48, 50, 52) sts rem. Continue knitting around without further shaping until sleeve is 14¼ (14¼, 14¾, 14¾) in / 36 (36, 37.5, 37.5) cm long or desired length. Change to smaller size dpn and work in k1, p1 ribbing for 2½ in / 6 cm. BO in ribbing. Make the second sleeve the same way.

FINISHING

Weave in all ends neatly on WS. Sew on buttons spaced as for buttonholes.

Chart Symbols

☐ = MC

■ = CC

Chart A

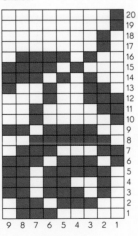

Chart B

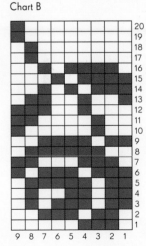

Sigrid
A classic pullover with Nordic pattern motifs

Sigrid is a simple and robust sweater that, thanks to the Icelandic wool yarn, protects against weather and wind. I decided to place several panels of Nordic motif-filled panels across the front, making the sweater even warmer because the yarn is doubled here.

SIZES S (M, L, XL, XXL, XXXL)

FINISHED MEASUREMENTS
Chest: 36¼ (36¼, 39½, 42½, 46½, 50½) in / 84 (92, 100, 108, 118, 128) cm
Length: 21¼ (22, 22¾, 23¾, 24½, 25¼) in / 54 (56, 58, 60, 62, 64) cm
Sleeve length: 17 (17¼, 17¾, 17¾, 18¼, 18½) in / 43 (44, 45, 45, 46, 47) cm

MATERIALS
Yarn: CYCA #4 (worsted/afghan/aran) Léttlopi from Ístex (100% Icelandic wool; 109 yd/100 m / 50 g)
Yarn Amounts:
  MC: 450 (500, 550, 600, 650, 700) g Almond Brown 1420
  CC: 100 (100, 100, 100, 100, 100) g White 0051

Needles: U.S. size 7 / 4.5 mm: straights and 16 in / 40 cm circular
Gauge: 19 sts x 21 rows in St st = 4 x 4 in / 10 x 10 cm. Adjust needle size to obtain correct gauge if necessary.

GARMENT CONSTRUCTION AND TECHNIQUES
The back, front, and sleeves are each worked back and forth and then sewn together. The neckband is knitted on last.

BACK
With MC and straight needles, CO 83 (87, 95, 103, 115, 123) sts and work back and forth in ribbing as follows:
Row 1 (WS): P3, (k1, p3) to end of row.
Row 2 (RS): K3, (p1, k3) to end of row.
Row 3: Work as for Row 1.
Rep Rows 2–3 until piece measures 2½ in / 6 cm. End with a WS row = Row 3). Now work in St st until piece measures 20 (21, 21¾, 22½, 23½, 23¼, 24) in / 51 (53, 55, 57, 59, 61) cm.
Shape back neck: BO the center 27 (27, 31, 31, 31, 33) sts for back neck and work each side separately. At neck edge, on every other row, BO 2 sts 3 times, and, *at the same time*, shape shoulder: BO 7 (8, 9, 10, 12, 13) sts 2 times and then 8 (8, 8, 10, 12, 13) sts. Fasten off rem st loop. Work the other side of neck to correspond.

FRONT
With MC and straight needles, CO 83 (87, 95, 103, 115, 123) sts and work back and forth in ribbing as follows:
Row 1 (WS): P3, (k1, p3) to end of row.
Row 2 (RS): K3, (p1, k3) to end of row.
Row 3: Work as for Row 1.
Rep Rows 2–3 until piece measures 2½ in / 6 cm. End with a WS row = Row 3). Now work 2 (2, 4, 4, 6, 6) rows in St st.
Work Charts A1 and A2 as a sequence (A1 + A2 combine

to go across the front—see garment photos).

NOTE: Stitch #42 (44, 48, 52, 58, 62) on Chart A1 is the center st of the front.

After completing Charts A1 and A2, continue to Charts B1 and B2 (sequenced across the front as for Charts A1 and A2). The piece should now measure 18¼ (19, 19¾, 20½, 21¼, 22) in / 46 (48, 50, 52, 54, 56) cm. Stitch #42 (44, 48, 52, 58, 62) is also the center front st, as for Charts A1 and A2.

Shape front neck: BO the center 17 (17, 21, 21, 21, 23) sts for front neck and work each side separately. At neck edge, on every other row, BO 2 sts 3 times, 2 sts 2 times, and 1 st once. Continue in St st until piece measures 20 (21, 21¾, 22½, 23¼, 24) in / 51 (53, 55, 57, 59, 61) cm.

Shape shoulder: BO 7 (8, 9, 10, 12, 13) sts 2 times and then 8 (8, 8, 10, 12, 13) sts. Fasten off rem st loop. Work the other side of neck to correspond.

SLEEVES

With MC and straight needles, CO 41 (43, 43, 45, 47, 47) sts and work back and forth in ribbing as follows:

Row 1 (WS): P0 (1, 1, 2, 3, 3), (k1, p3) across, ending with k1, p0 1, 1, 2, 3, 3).

Row 2 (RS): K0 (1, 1, 2, 3, 3), (p1, k3) across, ending with p1, k0 (1, 1, 2, 3, 3).

Chart A1

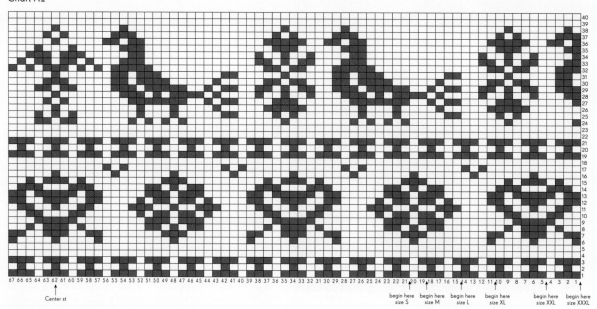

Chart A2

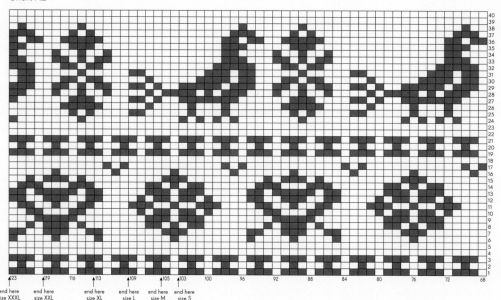

Chart Symbols

☐ := MC
■ := CC

Row 3: Work as for Row 1.

Rep Rows 2–3 until piece measures 2½ in / 6 cm.
Continue in St st until sleeve measures 2¾ (3¼, 1¼, 2¾, 2½, 4¼) in / 7 (8, 3, 7, 6, 11) cm.

Shape sleeves: Increase 1 st at each side inside an edge st: K1, M1, knit to last st, M1, k1. Increase the same way every 1¼ (1¼, 1¼, 1, 1, ¾) in / 3 (3, 3, 2.5, 2.5, 2) cm another 11 (11, 13, 14, 15, 17) times = 65 (67, 71, 75, 79, 83) sts.

When sleeve measures 17 (17¼, 17¾, 17¾, 18¼, 18½) in / 43 (44, 45, 45, 46, 47) cm, loosely BO all sts. Make the second sleeve the same way.

FINISHING

Join shoulder seams.

Neckband: With small circular and MC, pick up and knit 84 (84, 84, 88, 88, 88) sts around neck. Join, pm for beg of rnd, and work around in k3, p1 ribbing until until ribbing measures ¾ in / 2 cm. BO in ribbing.

Seam underarms. Sew side and sleeve seams. Weave in all ends neatly on WS.

Chart B1

Chart B2

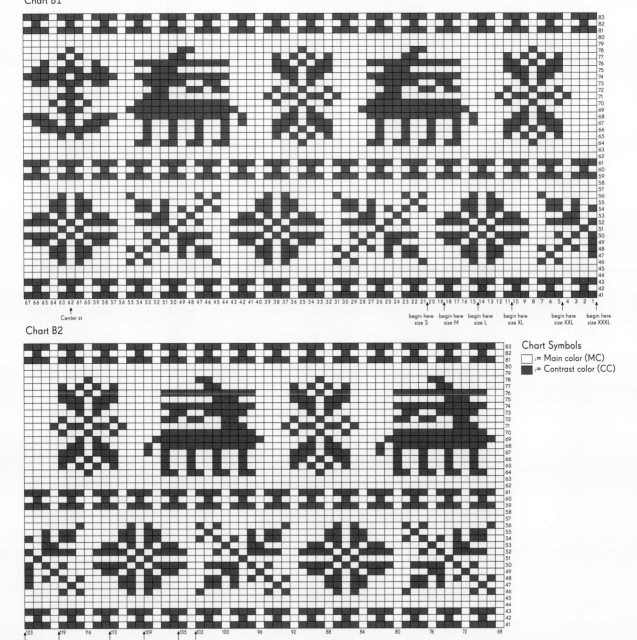

Chart Symbols

☐ := Main color (MC)

■ := Contrast color (CC)

Kajsa
Dress with patterned sleeves

I let the sleeves, with wide pattern bands on the lower sections, play the major role for this dress. Knitting a whole dress is something of a dream for many knitters. Kajsa is worked with a rustic wool yarn, which makes it a feasible project despite its size.

SIZES S (M, L, XL, XXL)

FINISHED MEASUREMENTS
Chest: 37¾ (41, 44, 48, 52) in / 96 (104, 112, 122, 132) cm
Length: 39 (40, 40½, 41, 41¼) in / 99 (101, 103, 104, 105) cm
Sleeve length: 18½ (19, 19¼, 19¼, 19¾) in / 47 (48, 49, 49, 50) cm

MATERIALS
Yarn: CYCA #4 (worsted/afghan/aran) Gästrike 4 ply from Järbo Garn (100% wool; 164 yd/150 m / 100 g)
Yarn Amounts:
MC: 1000 (1100, 1200, 1300, 1300) g Light Gray 9402

CC1: 100 g (all sizes) Natural White 9401
CC2: 100 g (all sizes) Dark Gray 9404
Notions: 1 stitch holder
Needles: U.S. sizes 7 and 8 / 4.5 and 5 mm: straights, 16 in / 40 cm circulars and, smaller size only, set of 5 dpn
Gauge: 20 sts x 24 rows in St st on larger needles = 4 x 4 in / 10 x 10 cm.
Adjust needle sizes to obtain correct gauge if necessary.

GARMENT CONSTRUCTION AND TECHNIQUES
The back and front, knitted separately, are worked back and forth while the sleeves are knitted in the round.

BACK
With MC and smaller needles, CO 110 (118, 126, 138, 146) sts. Work across in k2, p2 ribbing, ending with k2. Work subsequent ribbing rows with knit over knit and purl over purl until piece measures 4 in / 10 cm.
Change to larger needles and St st. On the first row, decrease evenly spaced across 0 (0, 0, 2, 0) sts = 110 (118, 126, 136, 146) sts. Work straight up in St st until piece measures 15¾ (15¾, 16¼, 16½, 16½) in / 40 (40, 41, 42, 42) cm.
Armhole shaping: Decrease 1 st at each side on a RS row as follows: K1, sl 1, k1, psso (see Knitting School, page 148) or dec with ssk. Knit until 3 sts rem and end with k2tog, k1. Decrease the same way every 1½ in / 4 cm 5 more times = 98 (106, 114, 124, 134) sts rem. Continue without shaping until piece measures 31 (31½, 32, 32¼, 32¼) in / 79 (80, 81, 82, 82) cm.
Raglan Sleeve Shaping: On every other row, dec at each side as follows: 3 (4, 5, 5, 6) sts once and then 2 sts 0 (1, 1, 2, 2) times. Dec 1 st at each side on every other row 27 (26, 26, 21, 21) times as follows: K2, ssk, knit until 4 sts rem, k2tog, k2.
Next, dec 2 sts on RS at each side on every other row 0 (1, 2, 6, 8) times as follows: K2, sk2p (= double dec: sl 1, k2tog, psso—see Knitting School, page 148), knit until 5 sts rem, k3tog (= 2 sts decreased), k2.

BO rem 38 (38, 40, 40, 40) sts.

FRONT

Work as for back but, when armhole measures 6¾ (7, 7½, 7½, 8) in / 17 (18, 19, 19, 20) cm, place the center 22 (22, 24, 24, 24) sts on a holder for the neck. Work each side separately.

At neck edge, BO 3 sts. Work 1 row and then, on the next row, BO 2 sts at neck edge. BO rem 3 sts. Work the other side of the neck the same way.

SLEEVES

With MC and smaller size dpn, CO 48 (50, 52, 54, 54) sts. Join, being careful not to twist cast-on row; pm for beg of rnd. Work around in k2, p2 ribbing for 2 in / 5 cm.

Change to larger size dpn and St st and work as follows:

Rnd 1: Knit.

Rnd 2: Increase 24 (22, 20, 18, 18) sts evenly spaced around. Inc with RLI (see Knitting School, page 148). There are now 72 sts for all sizes.

Rnd 3: Knit. Cut MC.

Now work following Chart A. With CC1 and CC2, work sts 1–48 and then 1–24. After completing Chart A, attach MC and knit 2 rnds. Next, increase with RLI 0 (0, 8, 8, 16) sts evenly space around = 72 (72, 80, 80, 88) sts. Knit 3 more rnds.

Now work Chart B, repeating it until the sleeve is 15¾ in / 40 cm long. Knit 1 rnd with MC. On the following rnd, adjust the stitch count, evenly spaced around, to 70 (74, 78, 82, 86) sts and then continue in St st with MC

until sleeve measures 18½ (19, 19¼, 19¼, 19¾) in / 47 (48, 49, 49, 50) cm.

Now work back and forth, shaping raglan as follows: At each side, BO 3 (4, 5, 5, 6) sts once and then 2 sts 0 (1, 1, 2, 2) times. Dec 1 st at each side on every other row 19 (17, 16, 17, 15) times and then 1 st on every 4th row 4 (5, 6, 5, 7) times as follows:

K2, ssk, knit until 4 sts rem, k2tog, k2. Loosely BO the rem 18 (18, 20, 20, 22) sts.

Make the second sleeve the same way.

FINISHING

Sew the raglan and side seams and then attach sleeves.

NECKBAND

With MC and smaller size circular, pick up and knit 92 (96, 96, 100, 100) sts around neck including those on holders. Pm for beg of rnd and work around in k2, p2 ribbing for ¾ in / 2 cm and then BO in ribbing. Weave in all ends neatly on WS.

Chart B

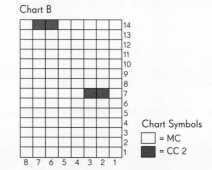

Chart A

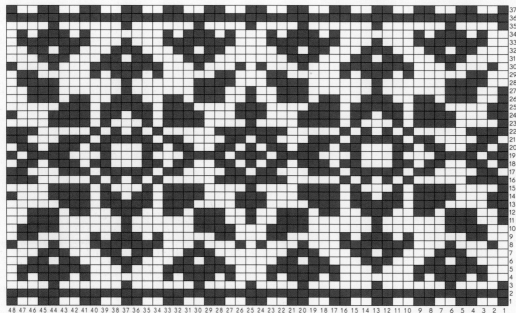

64

Esther
Reversible top with star patterns and buttons

Japanese costumes and textiles are decorated with simple, straight lines and ingenious details. I wanted to design something like that—and the result was the star-strewn Esther. You can wear it as a top buttoned down the back or as a sleeveless cardigan buttoned at the front.

SIZES S (M, L, XL, XXL, XXXL)

FINISHED MEASUREMENTS
Chest: 34¾ (37¾, 41, 45¾, 49¾, 54¼) in / 88 (96, 104, 116, 126, 138) cm
Length: 21¼ (21¼, 22, 22, 22¾, 22¾) in / 54 (54, 56, 56, 58, 58) cm

MATERIALS
Yarn: CYCA #3 (DK/light worsted) Hverdagsuld from Tusinfynd (100% wool; 164 yd/150 m / 50 g)

Yarn Amounts:
   MC: 200 (200, 250, 300, 350, 400) g Blue-green 02
   CC: 100 (100, 100, 100, 100, 100) g Natural White 28
Needles: U.S. sizes 4 and 6 / 3.5 and 4 mm: 32 in / 80 cm circulars and, in smaller size, set of 5 dpn
Notions: 7 (7, 8, 8, 8, 8) buttons (⅝ in / 15 mm in diameter); 4 stitch markers; 1 stitch holder
Gauge: 21 sts x 28 rows in St st on larger needles = 4 x 4 in / 10 x 10 cm.
Adjust needle sizes to obtain correct gauge if necessary.

GARMENT CONSTRUCTION AND TECHNIQUES
The sweater is worked back and forth on a circular needle, from the bottom up. The sleeves are worked in the round on double-pointed needles.

The raglan shaping worked on RS rows: *Knit until 3 sts rem before the marker, k2tog, k2, ssk* (or sl 1, k1, psso—see Knitting School, page 148). Rep * to * across.

Raglan shaping worked on WS rows: *Purl until 3 sts rem before the marker, p2tog tbl, p2, p2tog*. Rep * to * across.

The buttonholes are worked in the garter stitch bands over 5 sts: K2, k2tog, yo, k1. Buttonholes are worked along the first edge on the RS when the piece measures:

Size S: 2, 4¾, 7½, 10¼, 13, 15¾, 17¼ in / 5, 12, 19, 26, 33, 40 and 44 cm
Size M: 2, 4¾, 7½, 10¼, 13, 15¾, 17¼ in / 5, 12, 19, 26, 33, 40 and 44 cm
Size L: 2½, 4¾, 7, 9½, 11¾, 14¼, 16½, 18¼ in / 6, 12, 18, 24, 30, 36, 42, 46 cm
Size XL: 2½, 4¾, 7, 9½, 11¾, 14¼, 16½, 18¼ in / 6, 12, 18, 24, 30, 36, 42, 46 cm
Size XXL: 2, 4½, 7, 9½, 12¼, 14¾, 17¼, 19 in / 5, 11.5, 18, 24.5, 31, 37.5, 44, 48 cm
Size XXXL: 2, 4½, 7, 9½, 12¼, 14¾, 17¼, 19 in / 5, 11.5, 18, 24.5, 31, 37.5, 44, 48 cm

BODY

With MC and smaller size circular, CO 195 (213, 227, 251, 275, 299) sts. Work body back and forth.

Rows 1–7: Knit all rows (= garter st).

Row 8 (RS): Change to larger size circular and knit.

Row 9 (WS): K5, purl until 5 sts rem and end with k5.

NOTE: The 5 garter sts at each side are the button/buttonhole bands and are knitted in garter st throughout.

Rep Rows 8–9 a total of 1 (1, 3, 3, 5, 5) times.

Continue in St st, with the 5 sts in garter st at each side. Set up chart pattern on a RS row as follows: Button band, k1 (10, 5, 5, 5, 5), work following Chart A, sts 1–27. Rep sts 4–27 6 (6, 7, 8, 9, 10) times. Work Chart B (= 12 sts), k1 (10, 5, 5, 5, 5), knit button band. Work the chart rows 2 times total. *At the same time,* don't forget the buttonholes. Space buttonholes as indicated in the Garment Construction section above.

Finish with another 4 (4, 6, 6, 8, 8) rows in St st, adjusting the stitch count on the first of these rows to 196 (216, 228, 252, 276, 300) sts

On RS: K48 (53, 56, 62, 68, 74), BO 8 sts for armhole. Knit until you've worked 84 (94, 100, 112, 124, 136) sts after previous bind-off. BO 8 sts and knit to end of row.

There are now 84 (94, 100, 112, 124, 136) sts for the front and 48 (53, 56, 62, 68, 74) sts on each back piece. Set piece aside.

SLEEVES

With MC and smaller size dpn, CO 74 (78, 82, 86, 90, 94) sts and knit 7 rows in garter st.

Row 8: Knit and, *at the same time,* BO 4 sts at the beginning and end of the row = 8 sts total bound off and 66 (70, 74, 78, 82, 86) sts rem. Slip the sts to a stitch holder. Make the second sleeve the same way.

YOKE

Arrange the sleeves on the same circular as the body, matching at underarms = 312 (340, 360, 392, 424, 456) sts total. Pm at each intersection between sleeve and body = 4 markers. Continuing in St st, begin raglan shaping on the next (RS) row (see how to make the decreases in the Garment Construction section above) = 8 sts decreased per dec row.

Decrease as est on every other row a total of 20 (21, 22, 22, 23, 24) times and then on every row 3 (4, 5, 7, 8, 9) times = 128 (140, 144, 160, 176, 192) sts rem. Next, decrease 20 (30, 32, 45, 50, 58) sts evenly spaced across the row = 108 (110, 112, 115, 126, 134) sts rem.

Knit 3 rows in garter st. BO. Weave in all ends neatly on WS.

FINISHING

Seam the sleeves. Sew on buttons opposite buttonholes.

Chart A

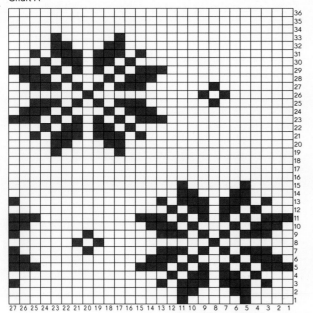

Chart B

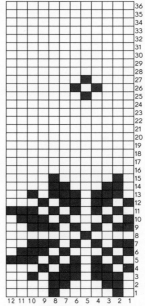

Chart Symbols
☐ = MC
■ = CC

Fredrika
Long cardigan with motifs from Öland

Fredrika, with its hidden pockets, is a cardigan you can curl up in on a cool autumn day. The ribbed sleeves and the loose fit leave room for layering underneath. If you want the sweater to close, just sew on four large snaps.

SIZES S (M, L, XL)

FINISHED MEASUREMENTS
Chest: 44 (49¾, 52¾, 57½) in / 112 (126, 134, 146) cm
Length: 30¾ (31½, 32¼, 33) in / 78 (80, 82, 84) cm
Sleeve length: 18½ (19¼, 19¾, 20) in / 47 (49, 50, 51) cm

MATERIALS
Yarn: CYCA #4 (worsted/afghan/aran) Alpakka Ull from Sandnes Garn (65% alpaca, 35% wool; 109 yd/ 100 m / 50 g)

Yarn Amounts:
   MC: 600 (650, 700, 750) g Beige 2650
   CC1: 100 g (all sizes) White 1002
   CC2: 100 g (all sizes) Petroleum 7572
Needles: U.S. size 8 / 5 mm: 40 in / 100 cm (or longer depending on size) circular and set of 5 dpn
Gauge: 20 sts x 25 rows in St st = 4 x 4 in / 10 x 10 cm. Adjust needle size to obtain correct gauge if necessary.

GARMENT CONSTRUCTION AND TECHNIQUES
The body and sleeves are worked back and forth on a long circular needle with each worked separately. The inset pockets are worked as part of the body using double-pointed needles.

BODY
With MC and long circular, CO 244 (266, 288, 310) sts and work in ribbing as follows:
Row 1 (WS): (P2, k1) until 2 sts rem; end p2.
Row 2 (RS): (K2, p1) until 2 sts rem; end k2.
Row 3: Work as for Row 1.
Rep Rows 2–3 until piece measures 4 in / 10 cm. End with a WS row.
Now work in St st except for 15 sts at each side which will continue in ribbing (= ribbed bands). *At the same time*, on the first row, inc 1 st in the St st section = 245 (267, 289, 311) sts. Work 1 more row.
Work following Chart A, Rows 1–32, changing the CC as shown in the photos: Rep sts 1–22 9 (10, 11, 12) times, and then sts 1–17 once = 1 row.

POCKETS
Place the first 30 (32, 35, 41) sts onto a holder. Place the next 21 sts onto a dpn, work 2 rows in St st with MC and CO 1 new edge st at each side. The edge sts

Chart B

    5 4 3 2 1
Rep 5 times

Chart Symbols
☐ = MC
■ = CC

are knitted with MC on all rows. Now work in St st and pattern following Chart B for the pocket, working back and forth until the pocket measures 11½ in / 29 cm.
End with 2 rows in MC, *at the same time* binding off the edge sts. Place the 21 sts back onto circular. Work the other pocket the same way. Place all held sts back onto circular.

BODY, CONTINUATION
Now work following Chart A, Rows 1–32.
Continue with MC until piece measures 21¾ in / 55 cm. From this point, the sections will be worked separately.

RIGHT FRONT
Work back and forth over the first 66 (70, 77, 82) sts = right front. When piece measures 22½ (23¼, 23¾, 28) in / 57 (59, 60, 71) cm, on RS, dec 1 st at front neck edge as follows: K15, k2tog, knit to end of row. Rep the dec row 20 (18, 21, 22) more times.
When the piece measures 28 (29½, 30¼, 31) in / 71 (75, 77, 79) cm, shape shoulder: from shoulder edge, on every other row:
Size S: BO 3 sts 2 times, 4 sts 6 times = 30 sts bound off.
Size M: BO 4 sts 4 times, 5 sts 4 times = 36 sts bound off.
Size L: BO 5 sts 8 times = 40 sts bound-off.
Size XL: BO 5 sts 4 times and 6 sts 4 times = 44 sts bound off.

Now only the 15-st ribbed band rem. CO 1 new st at the inner edge for a seam st = 16 sts and continue in ribbing for the band until, when stretched slightly, it reaches the center back neck on body. Place sts on a holder.

BACK
Work back and forth on the next 113 (127, 135, 147) body sts = back. When piece measures 28 (29½, 30¼, 31) in / 71 (75, 77, 79) cm, shape shoulders. On every other row, at each side:

Size S: BO 3 sts 2 times, 4 sts 6 times = 60 sts bound off.
Size M: BO 4 sts 4 times, 5 sts 4 times = 72 sts bound off.
Size L: BO 5 sts 8 times = 80 sts bound off.
Size XL: BO 5 sts 4 times and 6 sts 4 times = 88 sts bound off.

At the same time, when piece measures 28¼ (30, 30¾, 31½) in / 72 (76, 78, 80) cm, BO the center 17 (19, 19, 23) sts for back neck and work each side separately. At neck edge, on every other row, BO 5 sts 2 times, 2 sts 3 times, and 1 st 2 times = 36 sts bound off.

LEFT FRONT
Work back and forth over the rem 66 (70, 77, 82) sts of body = left front. When the piece measures 22½ (23¼, 23¾, 28) in / 57 (59, 60, 71) cm, on RS, dec 1 st at front neck edge as follows: Knit until 17 sts rem, ssk (or sl 1, k1, psso, see Knitting School, page 148), knit to end of row. Rep the dec row 20 (18, 21, 22) times.
When the piece measures 28 (29½, 30¼, 31) in / 71 (75, 77, 79) cm, shape shoulder: from shoulder edge, on every other row:
Size S: BO 3 sts 2 times, 4 sts 6 times = 30 sts bound off.
Size M: BO 4 sts 4 times, 5 sts 4 times = 36 sts bound off.
Size L: BO 5 sts 8 times = 40 sts bound-off.
Size XL: BO 5 sts 4 times and 6 sts 4 times = 44 sts bound off.

Now only the 15-st ribbed band rem. CO 1 new st at the inner edge for a seam st = 16 sts and continue in ribbing for the band until, when stretched slightly, it reaches the center back neck on body. Place sts on a holder.

Chart A

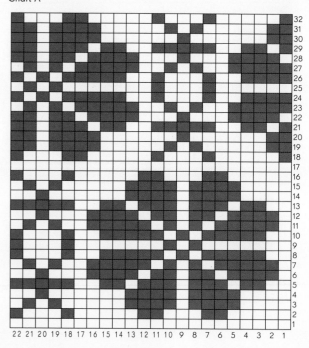

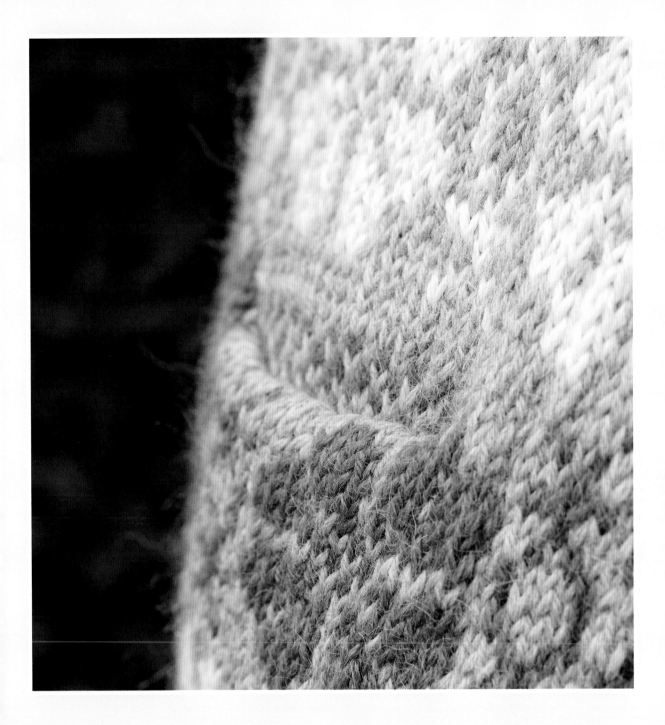

SLEEVES

With MC, CO 46 (49, 52, 52) sts and work in ribbing as
  follows:

Row 1 (WS): (K1, p2) until 1 st rem and end k1.

Row 2 (RS): (P1, k2) until 1 st rem and end p1.

Row 3: Work as for Row 1.

Rep Rows 2–3 until piece measures 1¼ (3½, 2¾, 1¼)
  in / 3 (9, 7, 3) cm. Now inc 1 st at each side (M1 inside an edge st). Rep the increase row 13 (15, 16, 18)
  more times, with 1¼ (1, 1, 1) in / 3 (2.5, 2.5, 2.5) cm

between each inc row = 74 (81, 86, 90) sts.

Continue in ribbing until sleeve measures 18½ (19¼,
  19¾, 20) in / 47 (49, 50, 51) cm. BO in ribbing.
  Make the second sleeve the same way.

FINISHING

Join shoulders. Use Kitchener st (see Knitting School,
page 149) to join ribbing at center back neck. Sew
band down along neck. Attach sleeves and sew sleeve
seams.

Greta
Cardigan with lice and floral-patterned yoke

Greta grew out of a floral pattern that, at one time, embellished a hat. The model begins and ends with a traditional lice pattern. The color combination reminds me of the colors of the primitive Värmland sheep.

SIZES S/M (L/XL, XXL)

FINISHED MEASUREMENTS
Chest: 35½ (42½, 51¼) in / 90 (108, 130) cm
Length: 19¾ (20½, 21¼) in / 50 (52, 54) cm
Sleeve length: 20½ (21, 21¼) in / 52 (53, 54) cm
Neck circumference: 22½ (24, 25) in / 57 (61, 63.5) cm

MATERIALS
Yarn: CYCA #1 (fingering) Finullgarn from Rauma (100% wool; 191 yd/175 m / 50 g)
Yarn Amounts:
  MC: 300 (350, 400) g White 401
  CC1: 50 g (all sizes) Dark Gray 405
  CC2: 100 g (all sizes) Brown 420

Notions: 9 buttons (⅝ in / 15 mm in diameter), 13-17 stitch markers (including 1 contrast color/style for beg of rnd), 1 stitch holder
Needles: U.S. sizes 1.5 and 2.5 / 2.5 and 3 mm: circulars and sets of 5 dpn
Gauge: 24-25 sts x 30 rows in St st with larger needles = 4 x 4 in / 10 x 10 cm.
Adjust needle sizes to obtain correct gauge if necessary.

GARMENT CONSTRUCTION AND TECHNIQUES
The cardigan is worked in the round from the top down on a circular needle—the yoke, body, and, finally, the sleeves. The front is steeked so it can be cut open up the center front afterwards. The button/buttonhole bands and neckband are knitted on afterwards.
M1R = Inc 1 st leaning to the right (see Knitting School, page 148).
M1L = Inc 1 st learning to the left (see Knitting School, page 148).
RLI = Inc 1 st into stitch below (see Knitting School, page 148).
Short Rows—see Knitting School, page 147.

YOKE
With CC1 and larger size circular, CO 138 (148, 154) sts (the 5 sts at center front are the steek for cutting open after the sweater has been knitted. Set up the 5 steek sts with 3 at the beginning of the round and 2 at the end). Join, being careful not to twist cast-on row; pm for beg of rnd.
NOTE: The first st (not included on chart) *before* Chart A is always knitted in the same color as the first st of Chart A.
Place markers after the first 3 sts and before the last 2 sts (steek) and pm between each charted pattern so it will be easy to see where the increases should be made.
Make sure you begin at the correct chart row for your size. Work Rows 5-60 (3-60, 1-60) on each of the charts, set up as follows: work Chart A and, as you work around the yoke, the other charts as follows: Chart B 4 (5, 6)

Chart A

Chart B

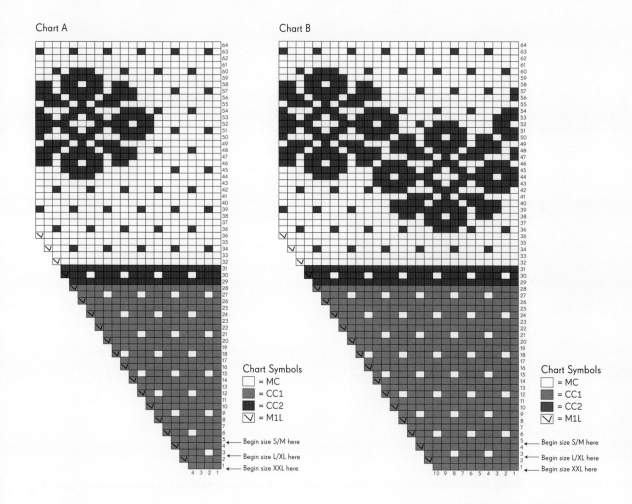

Chart Symbols

☐ = MC
▨ = CC1
■ = CC2
☑ = M1L

← Begin size S/M here
← Begin size L/XL here
← Begin size XXL here

times, Charts C and D, chart E 4 (5, 6) times and then finish with Chart F. *At the same time*, work the increases as indicated on the charts = 330 (386, 442) sts.

After completing the lice upper yoke and floral patterns, continue in lice pattern with the lice spaced as before. Work another 0 (6, 8) rnds. Remove markers.

BODY

K3 (= steek), k48 (57, 66) and place 68 (78, 84) sts on a holder (= sleeve sts).

CO 6 new sts, pm (= center of side) and then CO 6 new sts.

Work 93 (111, 137) sts and place 68 (78, 84) sts on a holder (= sleeve sts).

CO 6 new sts, pm (= center of side) and CO 6 new sts.

Work 48 (57, 66) sts, k2 (= steek) = 218 (254, 298) sts for body.

Continue in lice pattern and steek until piece measures 9½ (9¾, 10¼) in 24 (25, 26) cm.

Change to smaller size circular and work in k1, p1 ribbing for 1½ in / 4 cm. BO in ribbing.

SLEEVES

Continue the lice pattern, spaced as before.

Beg at center of underarm, pick up and knit 6 sts (where you had previously cast on new sts). K68, 78, 84 sts from holder, pick up and knit another 6 sts at underarm = 80 (90, 96) sts. Pm for beg of rnd.

Knit around in pattern until sleeve measures 2¾ (2, 2) in / 7 (5, 5) cm. As you decrease from this point, make sure that the lice continue to align.

Decrease Rnd: K1, ssk, knit until 3 sts rem and end k2tog, k1 = 2 sts decreased.

Rep the decrease rnd every 1½ (1¼, 1¼) in / 3.5 (3, 3) cm a total of 12 (15, 15) times = 24 sts decreased = 56 (60, 66) sts rem. The sleeve should measure 19 in / 48 cm.

Change to smaller size dpn and work around in k1, p1 ribbing for 1½ in / 4 cm. BO in ribbing.

Make the second sleeve the same way.

BUTTONBANDS

Reinforcing Steek: Machine-stitch (or use back stitch by hand) two lines on each side of the center steek st. Carefully cut the steek open down the center. The edges will roll in towards the WS.

Left Front, Button Band: With RS facing, MC and smaller needles, pick up and knit 113 (117, 121) sts along the left front. Work 12 rows in k1, p1 ribbing. BO in ribbing.

Chart C

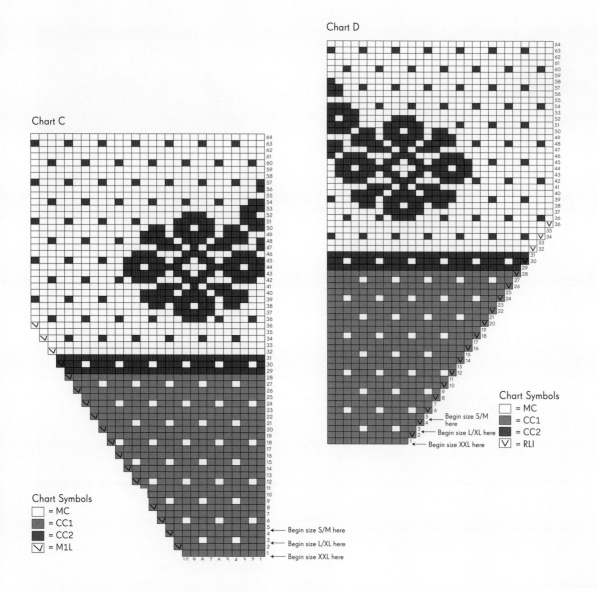

Chart D

Chart Symbols (Chart C)
- ☐ = MC
- ▨ = CC1
- ■ = CC2
- ⋁ = M1L

Begin size S/M here
Begin size L/XL here
Begin size XXL here

Chart Symbols (Chart D)
- ☐ = MC
- ▨ = CC1
- ■ = CC2
- ⋁ = RLI

Begin size S/M here
Begin size L/XL here
Begin size XXL here

Right Front, Buttonhole Band: With RS facing, MC and smaller needles, pick up and knit 113 (117, 121) sts along the right front. Work 5 rows in k1, p1 ribbing.

Buttonhole Row 1: Work 4 (6, 4) sts in ribbing, *BO 2 sts, work 11 (11, 12) sts in ribbing*; rep * to * 7 times, BO 2 sts, work 3 (5, 3) sts in ribbing.

Buttonhole Row 2: Work 3 (5, 3) sts in ribbing, CO 2 new sts, *work 11 (11, 12) sts in ribbing, CO 2 sts*; rep * to * 7 times, work 4 (6, 4) sts in ribbing.

Work 5 more rows in ribbing. BO in ribbing.

NECKBAND

With RS facing, MC, and smaller size circular, pick up and knit 131 (153, 175) sts evenly spaced around neck.

K37 (43, 49) and pm for beg of row.

Short Row 1: K57 (67, 77), wrap and turn.

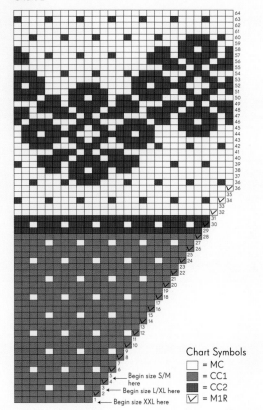

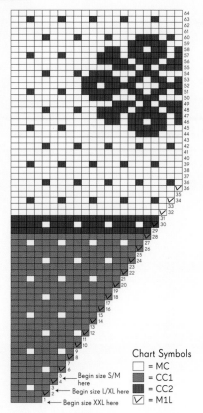

Short Row 2: K62 (72, 82), wrap and turn.
Short Row 3: K67 (77, 87), wrap and turn.
Short Row 4: K72 (82, 92), wrap and turn.
Short Row 5: K77 (87, 97), wrap and turn.
Short Row 6: Knit across all sts to center front.
Knit a complete row, but, *at the same time*, decrease 8 (10, 12) sts evenly spaced across = 123 (143, 163) sts rem.
Knit 5 rows. BO knitwise.

FINISHING

Sew on buttons opposite buttonholes. If desired, cover the cut edges of the steek with a decorative ribbon or fold the edge in and sew it down as invisibly as possible on the WS.

THE BOYFRIEND SWEATER CURSE AND THE FIANCÉ MISTAKE

My friend Carin knows a lot about old knitting myths. For example, a girl absolutely must not knit a sweater for her boyfriend because the relationship is bound to end before the sweater is finished. Socks and mittens are okay, but in those cases the knitter has to purposefully knit a little mistake into the pattern. Greta has a little "fiancé mistake"—can you spot it?

THE WHOLE ROW

My blog reader, Eva, told me that her grandmother taught her that one should never put aside knitting in the middle of a row because if you did, a sailor could drown! It is easy to imagine how this stricture came about—young girls were taught to avoid dropped stitches and pattern mistakes by finishing a row before setting a piece aside.

Kristin
Cardigan with flower panels

Kristin is my reconstruction of a fantastic sweater that my mother, Kajsa, bought in Dalarna and then gave to me. I have been as faithful to the original as possible, but have modernized the sweater's construction so it's knitted in one piece without seams.

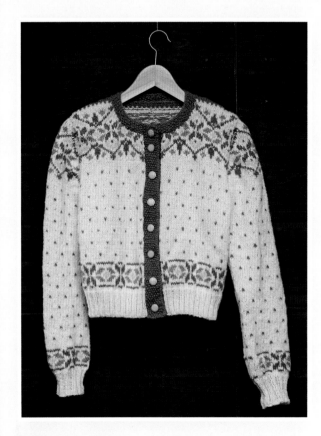

SIZES S (M, L/XL)

FINISHED MEASUREMENTS
Chest: 40¼ (42½, 47¼) in / 102 (108, 120) cm
Length: 18½ (19, 19) in / 47 (48, 48) cm
Sleeve length: 19¾ (19¾, 20¼) in / 50 (50, 51.5) cm

MATERIALS
Yarn: CYCA #3 (DK/light worsted) Hverdagsuld from Tusinfynd (100% wool; 164 yd/150 m / 50 g)
Yarn Amounts:
  MC: 300 (300, 350) g Natural White 28
  CC1: 100 g (all sizes) Medium Gray 07
  CC2: 50 g (all sizes) Old Rose 18
  CC3: 50 g (all sizes) Sea Grass 33
  CC4: 50 g (all sizes) Light Ochre 35

Needles: U.S. sizes 4 and 6 / 3.5 and 4 mm: 32 in / 80 cm circulars; smaller size: set of 5 dpn; larger size: 16 in / 40 cm circular
Notions: 8 buttons (½ in / 13 mm in diameter); 4 stitch markers
Gauge: 21 sts x 28 rows in St st on larger needles = 4 x 4 in / 10 x 10 cm.
Adjust needle sizes to obtain correct gauge if necessary.

GARMENT CONSTRUCTION AND TECHNIQUES
The sweater is worked back and forth on a circular needle, from the bottom up in one piece. The shoulders are seamed. The sleeves are worked from the top down by picking up and knitting stitches around the armhole. The armholes are shaped with short rows (see Knitting School, page 147). Finally, the front bands and neck band are knitted on.

Seed Stitch
Row 1: (K1, p1) across.
Row 2 and all following rows: Work purl over knit and knit over purl.

BODY
With MC and smaller size circular, CO 186 (198, 222) sts. Work back and forth in k2, p2 ribbing (= k2, p2 on RS and p2, k2 on WS) for 19 rows. On Row 19, pm between sts 45 and 46 (48 and 49; 54 and 55) = Marker 1; between sts 46 and 47 (49 and 50; 55 and 56) = Marker 2; between sts 141 and 142 (150 and 151; 168 and 169) = Marker 3; between sts 142 and 143 (151 and 152; 169 and 170) = Marker 4.

Change to larger size circular. Continue in St st except for the sts between Markers 1 and 2 and 3 and 4 which are always purled on the RS and knit on the WS (to form a false seam at each side). Work 2 rows.

Now work following Chart A, Rows 1-15: 45 (48, 54) sts at the point marked with 1, sl m (see Knitting School, page 150), k1, sl m. Work 95 (101, 113) sts at the point marked with 1 (2, 3), sl m, k1, sl m. Work 45 (48, 54) sts at the point marked with 4 (5, 6). Purl 1 row with MC.

Chart A

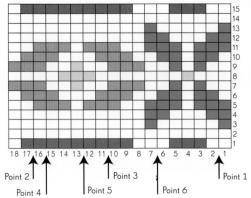

Point 2
Point 4
Point 5
Point 3
Point 6
Point 1

Chart Symbols
☐ = MC
■ = CC1
☐ = CC2
■ = CC3
■ = CC4

Chart B

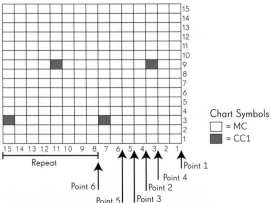

Repeat
Point 6
Point 5
Point 3
Point 2
Point 4
Point 1

Chart Symbols
☐ = MC
■ = CC1

Chart C

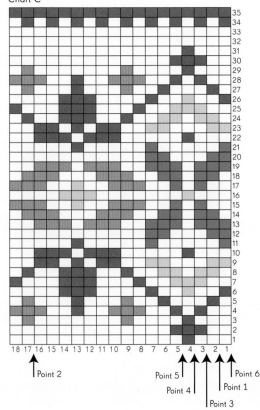

Point 2
Point 5
Point 4
Point 3
Point 1
Point 6

After completing Chart A, continue on to Chart B: 45 (48, 54) sts at the point marked with 1, sl m (see Knitting School, page 150), k1, sl m. Work 95 (101, 113) sts at the point marked with 2 (3, 4), sl m, k1, sl m. Work 45 (48, 54) sts at the point marked with 1 (5, 6). Work 3 rows.

On Row 5, inc 1 st before Marker 1, 1 st after Marker 2, 1 st before Marker 3, and 1 st after Marker 4 = 4 sts increased. Rep the increase row on every 5th row 3 times = 203 (215, 239) sts. Next, inc 1 st before Marker 1, and 1 st after Marker 4 on every 5th row 3 times = 209 (221, 245) sts.

NOTE: Continue pattern knitting while you work the increases.

Continue straight up until piece measures 10¾ in / 27 cm. End with a WS row so that the RS will be the next row. Now work each section separately. The stitches for the unworked sections will remain on the circular.

RIGHT FRONT

Shape Armhole

Work the 52 (55, 61) sts of the right front (continuing with the pattern on Chart B + the stitch between Markers 1 and 2 = 53 (56, 62) sts. Turn and BO the first 7 (8, 9) sts and then complete row = 46 (48, 53) sts rem.

Dec 1 st at armhole edge on the following 5 (5, 7) rows and then on every other row 2 (3, 3) times. Work 3 rows and then dec once more at armhole edge on the 4th row = 38 (39, 42) sts rem.

Work 2 (4, 4) rows without shaping.

Now work following Chart C beg at the point marked with 1 for 16 rows. Continue following the chart, and, *at the same time*, work the shaping for the neck and shoulder.

NOTE: After completing charted rows, continue with Gray until the piece is finished.

Shape Neck

BO 10 (9, 10) sts and complete row = 28 (30, 32) sts rem.

Dec 1 st at neck edge on each of the following 5 rows and then on every other row 2 (3, 3) times, and, finally, on every fourth row 2 times = 19 (20, 22) sts rem.

Shape Shoulder

On WS: BO 7 (7, 8) sts at beginning of row. Knit 1 row on RS.

BO another 6 (7, 8) sts at beginning of WS. Knit 1 row. BO the rem 6 sts. Cut yarn.

BACK
Shape Armholes

Now work on the 103 (109, 121) sts for the back as follows: BO 6 (7, 8) sts at the beginning of the next two rows = 91 (95, 105) sts rem.

Dec 1 st at each side on the next 5 (5, 7) rows and then on every other row 2 (3, 3) times. Work 3 rows and then dec 1 st at each armhole edge on the 4th row = 75 (77, 83) sts rem.

Work 2 (4, 4) rows.

Now work following Chart C, with the point marked with 3 (1, 2). The neck and shoulder shaping will occur as you work the charted rows, so please read next section of instructions before you start knitting.

NOTE: After completing charted rows, continue with Gray only.

Shape Back Neck and Shoulders

BO 7 (7, 8) sts at the beginning of each of the next two rows = 61 (63, 67) sts rem.

On next, RS, row: BO 7 (7, 8) sts and work until 10 (12, 12) sts rem. Turn and work each side separately.

BO 4 sts at the beginning of the next row and then BO the rem 6 (8, 8) sts on the following (last) row.

With RS facing you, work on the center section: BO 26 (24, 26) sts and then work another 17 (19, 20) sts.

Next row (WS): BO 7 (7, 8) sts at beginning of row.

BO 4 sts at the beginning of the next row and then BO the rem 7 (9, 9) sts on the next (last) row.

LEFT FRONT
Shape Armhole

Continue with the 1 st between Markers 3 and 4 and then the 52 (55, 61) sts of the left front = 53 (56, 62) sts. BO the first 7 (8, 9) sts (the first st bound off is also the st between Markers 3 and 4) and complete row = 46 (48, 53) sts rem.

Dec 1 st at armhole edge on the following 5 (5, 7) rows and then on every other row 2 (3, 3) times. Work 3 rows

and then dec once more at armhole edge on the 4th row = 38 (39, 42) sts rem.

Work 2 (4, 4) rows without shaping.

Now work following Chart C from the point marked with 5 (4, 6) for 16 rows. Continue following the chart, and, *at the same time*, work the shaping for the neck and shoulder.

NOTE: After completing charted rows, continue with Gray until the piece is finished.

Shape Neck

BO 10 (9, 10) sts and complete row = 28 (30, 32) sts rem.

Dec 1 st at neck edge on each of the following 5 rows and then on every other row 2 (3, 3) times, and, finally, on every fourth row 2 times = 19 (20, 22) sts rem.

Shape Shoulder

On RS: BO 7 (7, 8) sts at beginning of row. Work 1 row on WS. BO another 6 (7, 8) sts on WS. Knit 1 row. BO the rem 6 sts. Cut yarn.

Seam shoulders.

SLEEVES

The sleeves on this sweater are worked from the top down with stitches picked up and knitted along the armhole.

With RS facing and the starting point at center of underarm, in line with the false seam: with larger size circular and MC, pick up and knit 82 sts evenly spaced around the armhole. At the same time, place 4 markers: Marker 1 between sts 1 and 2; Marker 2 between sts 29 and 30; Marker 3 between sts 54 and 55; Marker 4 between sts 82 and 1.

NOTE: The st between Markers 4 and 1 is always purled on RS and knit on WS (to produce a false seam as at each side). Otherwise, work in St st with knit sts on RS and purl sts on WS.

Short Rows to Shape Sleeve Cap

Short Row 1 (RS): Knit to Marker 3; wrap st and turn.

Short Row 2 (WS): Purl to Marker 2; wrap and turn. Now begin working Chart D.

Short Row 3 (RS): Knit to Marker 3, pick up and knit the wrapped st from previous row; wrap and turn.

Short Row 4 (WS): Purl to Marker 2, pick up and knit the wrapped st from previous row; wrap and turn. Work new sts into Chart D pattern.

Continue short rows the same way—increase the short row

by 1 st at the end of every new row until 7 sts rem on each side of Markers 1 and 4. A total of 15 sts (7 + 1 + 7) sts are not included in the short rows.

Knit to Marker 4 and then begin working in the round (pm for beg of rnd at underarm seam). Work lice pattern spaced as on body and aligned as established by the lice at the top of Chart D. Work lice pattern into shaping, omitting lice that no longer fit into pattern.

Remove Markers 2 and 3 and knit 2 rnds.

Decrease Sequence 1: Sl Marker 1, k1, ssk, knit until 3 sts rem before Marker 4, k2tog, k1 = 2 sts decreased. Knit 3 rnds.

Rep * to * 6 times = 7 decrease rnds = 68 sts rem. Knit 4 rnds.

Decrease Sequence 2: Sl Marker 1, k1, ssk, knit until 3 sts rem before Marker 4, k2tog, k1 = 2 sts decreased. Knit 7 rnds. Rep from * to * 4 times = 5 more decrease rnds = 58 sts rem.

Continue without further shaping until sleeve measures 15½ (15½, 16) in / 39 (39, 40.5) cm.

Now work following Chart A from the point marked with 1. **NOTE:** Continue the false seam st in purl and not in pattern. Knit 1 rnd.

Now decrease 22 (18, 18) sts evenly spaced around = 36 (40, 40) sts rem.

With smaller size dpn, work in k2, p2 ribbing over rem sts (including false seam) for 2½ in / 6 cm. BO in ribbing.

BUTTON/BUTTONHOLE BANDS

With CC1, larger needles, and RS facing you, pick up and knit 79 (81, 81) sts along left front.

Work in Seed st for 11 rows and then BO knitwise.

With CC1, larger needles, and RS facing you, pick up and knit 79 (81, 81) sts along right front.

Work in Seed st for 5 rows.

Buttonhole Row 1 (RS): Work 3 (4, 4) sts in Seed st, *BO 2 sts, work 10 sts in Seed st*. Rep * to * 5 times and then BO 2 sts, work 2 (3, 3) sts in Seed st.

Buttonhole Row 2 (WS): Work 2 (3, 3) sts in Seed st, *CO 2 sts, work 10 sts in Seed st*. Rep * to * 5 times and then CO 2 sts, work 3 (4, 4) sts in Seed st.

Work 4 more rows in Seed st. BO knitwise.

NECKBAND

With CC1, larger needles, and RS facing you, pick up and knit 79 (83, 83) sts evenly spaced around neck. Work 3 rows in Seed st.

Buttonhole Row 1 (RS): Work 3 sts in Seed st, *BO 2 sts, complete row in Seed st.

Buttonhole Row 2 (WS): Work in Seed st over 74 (78, 78) sts, CO 2 sts, complete row in Seed st.

Work 4 more rows in Seed st and then BO knitwise.

FINISHING

Weave in all ends neatly on WS. Sew on button opposite buttonholes.

Chart D

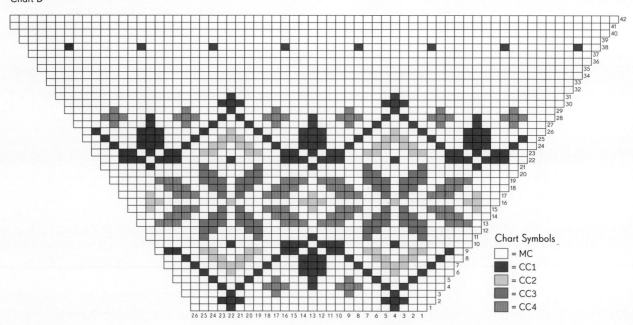

Chart Symbols

☐ = MC
■ = CC1
▨ = CC2
▨ = CC3
▨ = CC4

Hulda
Pullover with star-studded yoke

With Hulda, I wanted to sing the praises of simplicity with a little panel at the center. The color scale of the sweater reflects lonely forests and barren heather-covered moors. The silhouette of this design was inspired by the 1960s, with thoughts of the sweaters worn by Malin on Saltkråkan (a fictional island created by Astrid Lindgren for a television series).

SIZES S (MS, M, ML, L, XL, XXL)

FINISHED MEASUREMENTS
Chest: 34¾ (36¾, 38½, 41¼, 43¼, 45¼, 47¼) in / 88 (93, 98, 105, 110, 115, 120) cm
Length: 24 (24, 24, 24, 24, 24, 24½) in / 61 (61, 61, 61, 61, 61, 62) cm
Sleeve length: 15¾ (15¾, 16½, 16½, 17, 17, 17) in / 40 (40, 42, 42, 43, 43, 43) cm

MATERIALS
Yarn: CYCA #2 (sport/baby) Tove from Sandnes Garn (100% wool; 175 yd/160 m / 50 g)

Yarn Amounts:
    MC: 300 (300, 350, 350, 400, 450, 450) g Natural Heather 2641
    CC1: 100 g (all sizes) Heather 4342
    CC2: 100 g (all sizes) Charcoal Heather 1088
Needles: U.S. size 4 / 3.5 mm: 24 in / 60 cm circular and set of 5 dpn
Gauge: 24 sts x 30 rows in St st = 4 x 4 in / 10 x 10 cm. Adjust needle size to obtain correct gauge if necessary.

GARMENT CONSTRUCTION AND TECHNIQUES
The pullover is worked from the bottom up. The body and sleeves are worked separately and then joined for the yoke.
M1R—make 1 right-leaning increase (see Knitting School, page 148).
M1L—make 1 left-leaning increase (see Knitting School, page 148)

BODY
With MC and circular, CO 212 (224, 236, 252, 264, 276, 288) sts. Join, being careful not to twist cast-on row; pm for beg of rnd. Work around in k1, p1 ribbing for 18 rnds.
Change to St st and work around until body measures 15¾ (15¾, 15¾, 15½, 15½, 15½, 15½) in / 40 (40, 40, 39, 39, 39, 39) cm.
Shape armholes: BO 3 (3, 4, 4, 4, 4, 4) sts, k100 (106, 110, 118, 124, 130, 136), BO 6 (6, 8, 8, 8, 8, 8) sts, k100 (106, 110, 118, 124, 130, 136), BO 3 (3, 4, 4, 4, 4, 4) sts = 200 (212, 220, 236, 248, 260, 272) sts rem. Set body aside while you make sleeves.

SLEEVES
With MC and dpn, CO 44 (48, 48, 52, 52, 54, 54) sts. Divide sts as evenly as possible onto dpn and join. Knit around in k1, p1 ribbing for 18 rnds.
Change to St st and increase 2 sts (see details below)

every 6th (6th, 6th, 6th, 5th 4th, 4th) rnd a total of 16 (15, 17, 18, 22, 23, 24) times = 76 (78, 82, 88, 96, 100, 102) sts.

Increases: K1, M1L (see above), knit until 1 st rem, M1R (see above), k1.

After completing increases, continue in St st until sleeve measures 15¾ (15¾, 16½, 16½, 17, 17, 17) in / 40 (40, 42, 42, 43, 43, 43) cm

Shape Underarm: BO the first and last 3 (3, 4, 4, 4, 4) sts of next rnd = 70 (72, 74, 80, 88, 92, 94) sts rem.

YOKE

Place the sts from the body and sleeve onto circular with the underarms matching = 340 (356, 368, 396, 424, 444, 460) sts. The rnd now begins at the intersection between the right sleeve and the right side of the back.

Work in St st and, as necessary for stitch count, increase 0 (1, 6, 0, 1, 0, 0) sts or decrease 0 (0, 0, 5, 0, 2, 1) sts evenly spaced over the first rnd = 340 (357, 374, 391, 425, 442, 459) sts. Knit 6 rnds.

Decrease Rnd 1: (K15, k2tog) around = 320 (336, 352, 368, 400, 416, 432) sts. Knit 5 (5, 5, 6, 6, 6, 6) rnds St st.

Decrease Rnd 2: (K14, k2tog) around = 300 (315, 330, 345, 375, 390, 405) sts. Knit 5 (5, 5, 6, 6, 6, 6) rnds St st.

Decrease Rnd 3: (K13, k2tog) around = 280 (294, 308, 322, 350, 364, 378) sts. Knit 3 (3, 3, 3, 3, 6, 6) rnds St st.

Decrease Rnd 4: (K12, k2tog) around = 260 (273, 286, 299, 325, 338, 351) sts. Knit 3 (3, 3, 3, 3, 3, 6) rnds St st.

Decrease Rnd 5: (K11, k2tog) around = 240 (252, 264, 276, 300, 312, 324) sts. Knit 3 rnds St st.

Decrease Rnd 6: (K10, k2tog) around = 220 (231, 242, 253, 275, 286, 297) sts. Knit 3 rnds St st.

Decrease Rnd 7: (K9, k2tog) around = 200 (210, 220, 230, 250, 260, 270) sts. Knit 3 rnds St st.

Decrease Rnd 8: *K23 (103, 16, 36, 7, 11, 7), k2tog)*; rep * to * until 0 (0, 4, 2, 16, 0, 0) ss rem; k0 (0, 4, 2, 16, 0, 0) = 192 (208, 208, 220, 224, 240, 240) sts.

Now work Rows 1–17 of Chart A.

On Row 18 of chart, decrease as follows: (K3, k2tog) until 12 (8, 8, 4, 4, 0, 0) sts rem, k12 (8, 8, 4, 4, 0, 0) = 156 (168, 168, 180, 180, 192, 192 sts rem.

Work Rows 1–3 of Chart B. Cut CC1 and CC2 and attach MC. Knit 3 rnds.

On the next rnd, decrease as follows: *K7 (4, 5, 3, 4, 3, 3), k2tog*; rep * to * until 12 (0, 0, 10, 0, 2, 2) sts rem. K12 (0, 0, 10, 0, 2, 2) = 140 (140, 144, 146, 150, 154, 154) sts rem.

Work 6 rnd in k1, p1 ribbing and then BO in ribbing.

FINISHING

Seam underarms with Kitchener stitch (see Knitting School, page 149). Weave in all ends neatly on WS.

Chart A

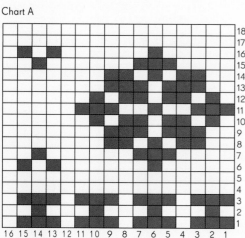

18
17
16
15
14
13
12
11
10
9
8
7
6
5
4
3
2
1

16 15 14 13 12 11 10 9 8 7 6 5 4 3 2 1

Chart Symbols

☐ = CC1
■ = CC2

Chart B

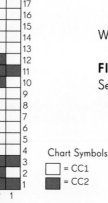

3
2
1

4 3 2 1

Kerstin
Stole with eight-petaled roses

Combining knitted garments with shiny or sheer party fabrics such as silk or tulle produces an exciting dynamic. So, I wanted to create a stole that shows the magnificence of our Swedish pattern tradition to wear for a special party or bride's dress.

Adjust needle size to obtain correct gauge if necessary.

GARMENT CONSTRUCTION AND TECHNIQUES
The stole is knitted in two pieces, each worked back and forth, that are then grafted down the back. The garment is finished with a ribbed edge at the sides.

RIGHT PIECE
**With MC and circular, CO 75 sts.
Row 1 (WS): (P3, k1) until 3 sts rem, end p3.
Row 2 (RS): (K3, p1) until 3 sts rem, end k3.
Row 3 (WS): (P3, k1) until 3 sts rem, end p3.
Rep Rows 2–3 until piece measures 1½ in / 4 cm.
Work 2 rows in St st**.
Now work following Chart A.
After completing charted rows, continue in St st with MC until piece measures 24¾ in / 63 cm. Slip the sts to a stitch holder or a length of yarn and set aside.

LEFT PIECE
Rep from ** to **.
Now work following Chart B.

SIZES One size

FINISHED MEASUREMENTS
Length: 49¾ in / 126 cm
Width: 15¾ in / 40 cm

MATERIALS
Yarn: CYCA #5 (bulky) Ulla from Järbo Garn (100% wool; 82 yd/75 m / 50 g)
Yarn Amounts:
  MC: 350 g Gray 26104
  CC: 50 g White 26106
Notions: 1 stitch holder, 1 metal clasp
Needles: U.S. size 8 / 5 mm: 32 in / 80 cm circular
Gauge: 18-19 sts x 23-24 rows in St st = 4 x 4 in / 10 x 10 cm.

After completing charted rows, continue in St st with MC until piece measures 24¾ in / 63 cm.

Graft both pieces with Kitchener stitch using MC (see Knitting School, page 149).

RIBBED EDGING

With RS facing, circular and MC, pick up and knit 187 sts along one long edge. Pick up 3 sts for every 4 rows. Work in ribbing as follows:

Row 1 (WS): (P3, k1) until 3 sts rem, end p3.
Row 2 (RS): (K3, p1) until 3 sts rem, end k3.
Row 3 (WS): (P3, k1) until 3 sts rem, end p3.

Rep Rows 2–3 until ribbing measures 1½ in / 4 cm.

BO in ribbing.

Work a ribbed edging along the other long side the same way.

FINISHING

Weave in all ends neatly on WS. Securely sew clasp on ribbing, aligned with the top of the patterning (see photo to left).

Chart A

Chart B

Chart Symbols
☐ = MC
■ = CC

Ragnhild
Poncho with diamond pattern

Ragnild is a poncho for nighttime in its warming alpaca yarn. By cutting off and disrupting a detail from an Öland pattern panel, I created a rhomboid pattern also associated with the Inca culture's pattern heritage.

SIZES One size

FINISHED MEASUREMENTS
Length: 15½ in / 39 cm
Circumference around shoulders: 39½ in / 100 cm

MATERIALS
Yarn: CYCA #5 (bulky) Suri Alpakka (Suri Alpaca) from Sandnes Garn (96% baby alpaca, 4% polyamide; 142 yd/130 m / 50 g)
AND CYCA #4 (worsted/afghan/aran) Alpakka Ull (Alpaca Wool) from Sandnes Garn (65% alpaca, 35% wool; 109 yd/100 m / 50 g)
Yarn Amounts:
  MC: Suri Alpakka—100 g Gray 1042
  CC1: Alpakka Ull—50 g Purple 4855
  CC2: Alpakka Ull—50 g Mustard Yellow 2035
  CC3: Alpakka Ull—50 g White 1002
Needles: U.S. size 8 / 5 mm : 24 in / 60 cm circular
Gauge: 16 sts x 21 rows in St st = 4 x 4 in / 10 x 10 cm.
Adjust needle size to obtain correct gauge if necessary.

GARMENT CONSTRUCTION AND TECHNIQUES
The poncho is knitted in the round in one piece from the top down.
RLI = Right-lifted increase (see Knitting School, page 148)

PONCHO
With MC and circular needle, CO 90 sts. Join, being careful not to twist cast-on row; pm for beginning of rnd. Work 4 rnds in St st (= knit all rnds).
Now increase for shoulders:
Increase Rnd 1: (K6, RLI) 15 times = 105 sts.
Knit 3 rnds.
Increase Rnd 2: (K7, RLI) 15 times = 120 sts.
Knit 3 rnds.
Increase Rnd 3: (K8, RLI) 15 times = 135 sts.
Knit 3 rnds.
Increase Rnd 4: (K9, RLI) 15 times = 150 sts.
Knit 3 rnds.
Increase Rnd 5: (K8, RLI, k7, RLI) 10 times = 170 sts.
Knit 6 rnds.
Change to CC3 and knit 3 rnds.
Now work following Chart A with CC2 and CC3.
Knit 3 rnds with CC3.
Next, work following Chart A with CC1 and CC3.
Knit 3 rnds with CC3.
Cut CC yarns and continue with MC only. Work in St st until piece measures 13 in / 33 cm. Now work in k2, p2 ribbing around until ribbing measures 2½ in / 6 cm.
BO loosely in ribbing. Cut yarn and weave in all ends neatly on WS.

Chart A

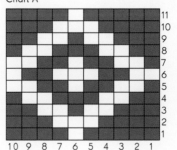

Flora
Arm warmers with flower motifs

Instead of a whole sweater, you can knit arm warmers and match them with a short-sleeved garment from your wardrobe. Thanks to well-placed increases, these long cuffs fit especially well. The pattern motif is a small segment from an old 1930s pattern.

SIZES S/M (L/XL)

FINISHED MEASUREMENTS
Length: 13¾ in / 35 cm
Circumference at wrist: 7 (9) in / 18 (23) cm
Circumference at elbow: 10¼ (12¼) in / 26 (31) cm

MATERIALS
Yarn: CYCA #5 (bulky) Ulla from Järbo Garn (100% wool; 82 yd/75 m / 50 g)
Yarn Amounts:
    MC: 100 g Natural White 26106
    CC1: 50 g Green 26109
    CC2: 50 g Rose 26121
    CC3: 50 g Purple 26122
Notions: 1 stitch marker
Needles: U.S. sizes 6 and 7 / 4 and 4.5 mm: sets of 5 dpn
Gauge: 18 sts x 21 rows in St st on larger needles = 4 x 4 in / 10 x 10 cm.
Adjust needle sizes to obtain correct gauge if necessary.

GARMENT CONSTRUCTION AND TECHNIQUES
The arm warmers are knitted around on double-pointed needles, from the bottom up.
Increases: Work as RLI—right-lifted increase (see Knitting School, page 148.

ARM WARMERS
With MC and smaller size dpn, CO 36 (44) sts; divide the sts evenly over the dpn. Join and pm for beginning of rnd.
Work around in k1, p1 ribbing for 4 in / 10 cm.
Change to larger size dpn and continue in St st (knit all rnds).
Knit 3 rnds.
Now work following Chart A with MC and CC1.
Knit 3 rnds with MC.
Increase Rnd 1: Inc 4 (6) sts evenly spaced around = 40 (50) sts.
Knit 1 rnd.

Work following Chart B with MC and CC2.
Knit 3 rnds.
Increase Rnd 2: Inc 2 (6) sts evenly spaced around = 42 (56) sts.
Knit 1 rnd.
Work following Chart C with MC and CC1.
Knit 3 rnds.
Increase Rnd 3: Inc 6 (0) sts evenly spaced around = 48 (56) sts.
Knit 1 rnd.
Work following Chart D with MC and CC3.
Knit 3 rnds.
Increase Rnd 4: Inc 2 (4) sts evenly spaced around = 50 (60) sts.
Knit 1 rnd.
Work following Chart E with MC and CC1.
Knit 1 rnd.
Increase Rnd 5: Inc 4 (4) sts evenly spaced around = 54 (64) sts.
Change to smaller size dpn. Work around in k1, p1 ribbing until ribbed cuff measures 2 in / 5 cm.
BO in ribbing. Weave in all ends neatly on WS.
Make the second arm warmer the same way.

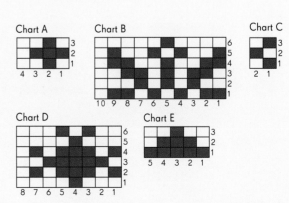

Johanna
Wrist warmers with Dala patterns

I gave the pretty Dala pattern a discreet framing by creating a simple and comfortable cuff. The garter stitch section in the middle allows the cuffs to be worn either stretched out or with a little pouf at the center.

SIZES XS/S (M/L)

FINISHED MEASUREMENTS
Length: 6¼ in / 16 cm
Wrist Circumference: 5¾ (7) in / 14.5 (18) cm

MATERIALS
Yarn: CYCA #1 (fingering) Engleuld from Tusinfynd (70% wool, 30% baby alpaca; 252 yd/230 m / 50 g)
Yarn Amounts:
10 g each of:
    CC1: Dark Petroleum 24
    CC2: Blue-Green 22
    CC3: Dark Raspberry 17
    CC4: Old Rose 14
Needles: U.S. size 1.5 / 2.5 mm: set of 5 dpn
Gauge: 35 sts x 38 rows in St st = 4 x 4 in / 10 x 10 cm.
Adjust needle size to obtain correct gauge if necessary.

GARMENT CONSTRUCTION AND TECHNIQUES
The cuffs are worked in the round on double-pointed needles, from the bottom up.

WRIST WARMERS
With CC1 and dpn, CO 54 (66) sts. Divide onto dpn as evenly as possible and join.
Work around:
*Rnd 1: Knit.
Rnd 2: Purl
Rnd 3: Knit.
Rnd 4: Purl.
Rnd 5: Knit*.
Change to CC2 and knit 1 rnd.
Next, work following Chart A with CC1 and CC2.
After completing charted rows, knit 1 rnd with CC2.
Change to CC1.
Rep from * to *.
Change to CC3.
Rep from * to *.
Knit 1 rnd with CC4.
Work following Chart A with CC3 and CC4.
After completing charted rows, knit 1 rnd with CC4.
Change to CC3.
Rep from * to *.
BO. Weave in all ends neatly on WS. Make the second wrist warmer the same way.

Chart A

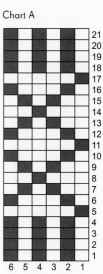

Elsa
Half gloves with country motifs

The Elsa half gloves are thin but nonetheless warm. You can easily substitute other motifs on these. If you want to substitute something else for this Västmanland pattern, all you have to do is look in the Pattern Library (pages 127–144) for a motif with a multiple of eight stitches.

SIZE One size

FINISHED MEASUREMENTS
Length: 8¾ in / 22 cm
Hand Circumference: 9 in / 23 cm

MATERIALS
Yarn: CYCA #1 (fingering) Finullgarn from Rauma (100% wool; 191 yd/175 m / 50 g)
Yarn Amounts:
   MC: 50 g Gray Blue 4287
   CC1: 50 g White 401
   CC2: 50 g Raspberry Red 439
Needles: U.S. sizes 1.5 and 2.5 / 2.5 and 3 mm: sets of 5 dpn
Gauge: 26 sts x 30 rows in St st on larger needles = 4 x 4 in / 10 x 10 cm.
Adjust needle sizes to obtain correct gauge if necessary.

GARMENT CONSTRUCTION AND TECHNIQUES
The cuffs are worked in the round on double-pointed needles, from the top down.

RIGHT HALF GLOVE
With MC and smaller size dpn, CO 56 sts. Divide sts evenly onto dpn and join. Work around in k2, p2 ribbing for 2 in / 5 cm.
Change to larger size dpn and St st (= knit on all rnds). Knit 2 rnds.
Thumbhole: K12 and place sts on a holder. Knit to end of rnd.
CO 12 new sts over the gap and complete rnd = 56 sts. Knit 2 more rnds.
Now work around following Chart A, working Rows 1–8 of chart a total of 3 times.
Cut CC yarns and continue with MC only. Knit 6 rnds.
Change to smaller size dpn and work in k2, p2 ribbing for 2 in / 5 cm. BO in ribbing. Cut yarn and weave in ends neatly on WS.

THUMB
Place the 12 held sts onto a smaller size dpn and then use another dpn and MC to pick up and knit 12 sts across the cast-on sts of thumbhole.
Work around in k2, p2 ribbing for 1¼ in / 3 cm. BO in ribbing. Cut yarn and weave in ends neatly on WS.

LEFT HALF GLOVE
Work as for right glove *but* place the last (instead of first) 12 sts of rnd on a holder for the thumb.

Chart A

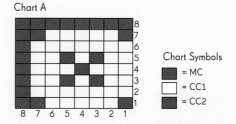

Chart Symbols
■ = MC
□ = CC1
■ = CC2

Lisa
Hat with motifs from the island of Öland

This classic hat, Lisa, is an excellent choice for beginners at two-color stranded knitting. The pattern is from Öland and is easy to knit because the color changes are so close that the yarns never need to be twisted around each other. You can pair the hat with Maja, the matching cowl, on page 105.

SIZE One size

FINISHED MEASUREMENTS
Circumference: 16½ in / 42 cm
Length: 9¾ in / 25 cm

MATERIALS
Yarn: CYCA #4 (worsted/afghan/aran) Alpakka Ull (Alpaca Wool) from Sandnes Garn (65% alpaca, 35% wool; 109 yd/100 m / 50 g)
Yarn Amounts:
MC: 50 g White 1002
CC: 50 g Petroleum 7572
Needles: U.S. sizes 7 and 8 / 4.5 and 4 mm: 16 in / 40 cm circulars and, larger needles only, set of 5 dpn
Gauge: 18 sts x 24 rows in St st on larger needles = 4 x 4 in / 10 x 10 cm.
Adjust needle sizes to obtain correct gauge if necessary.

GARMENT CONSTRUCTION AND TECHNIQUES
The hat is worked in the round, from the bottom up. When stitches no longer fit around circular, change to dpn.

HAT
With MC and smaller size circular, CO 94 sts. Join, being careful not to twist cast-on row; pm for beginning of rnd. Work around in k1, p1 ribbing for 3¼ in / 8 cm.
Change to larger size circular and St st. Increase on the first rnd: K3, *k11, M1*. Rep * to * until 3 sts rem and end with k3 = 102 sts. Knit 1 more rnd.
Now work following Chart A. Rep Rows 1–8 of chart until hat measures 8 in / 20 cm.

Chart A

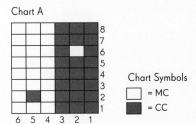

Chart Symbols
☐ = MC
■ = CC

Next, work following Chart B, working the decreases as indicated on chart = 34 sts rem.
Cut yarn, leaving a 6 in / 15 cm tail. Draw end through rem sts; tighten and fasten off.

Chart B

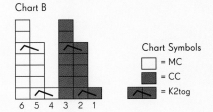

Chart Symbols
☐ = MC
■ = CC
⤙ = K2tog

POMPOM
Make a classic pompom with a 2¾ in / 7 cm diameter.

FINISHING
Securely sew the pompom to the top of the hat. Weave in all ends neatly on WS.

Maja
Cowl with Motifs from the island of Öland

This easily-knitted cowl can be worn single or double because it's essentially a long circularly-knit tube that's sewn into a circle. Maja, which has my name, has a pattern that matches Lisa, the hat on page 103.

SIZE One size

FINISHED MEASUREMENTS
Length: 47¼ in / 120 cm
Width: 8¾ in / 22 cm

MATERIALS
Yarn: CYCA #1 (fingering) Gästrike 2 ply from Järbo Garn (100% wool; 327 yd/299 m / 100 g)
Yarn Amounts:
  MC: 150 g White 9201
  CC: 150 g Purple 9208
Needles: U.S. size 2.5 / 3 mm: 16 in / 40 cm circular for knitting and an extra circular for finishing
Gauge: 25 sts x 36-37 rows in St st = 4 x 4 in / 10 x 10 cm.
Adjust needle size to obtain correct gauge if necessary.

GARMENT CONSTRUCTION AND TECHNIQUES
The cowl is knitted as a tube in stockinette on a short circular needle. It is knit on all rounds.

COWL
With MC, CO 120 sts with a crocheted provisional cast-on (see Knitting School, page 150). Join, being careful not to twist cast-on; pm for beginning of rnd.
Knit 1 rnd.
**Work following Chart A, working Rows 1-13. The motif is repeated 12 times around the tube.
Next, work Chart B (the motif repeats 20 times around). Repeat the 8 rows of Chart B until piece is about 21 in / 53 cm long. End after a complete repeat + Row 1 of chart.
Now work Chart A again, working Rows 12-13 and then Rows 1-11. End with 2 knit rnds with MC.**
Knit 2 rnds with CC.
Rep from ** to ** once, but, mirror image the colors.
End with 1 knit rnd with MC.
Carefully remove waste yarn from provisional cast-on and place sts on second circular.
Use Kitchener stitch to join the sets of stitches (see Knitting School, page 149).
Cut yarn and weave in all ends to WS.

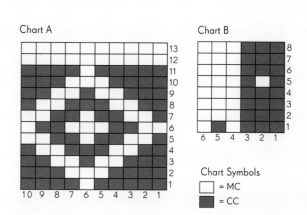

Chart A

Chart B

Chart Symbols
☐ = MC
■ = CC

Edith
Bag and leg warmers with motifs from Gästrike

Accessories are relatively quick to knit. The leg warmers and bag are both worked in the round, which makes the two-color stranded knitting simpler. You can easily substitute another motif—look in the Pattern Library (pages 127-144) and pick out a motif with a multiple of six stitches.

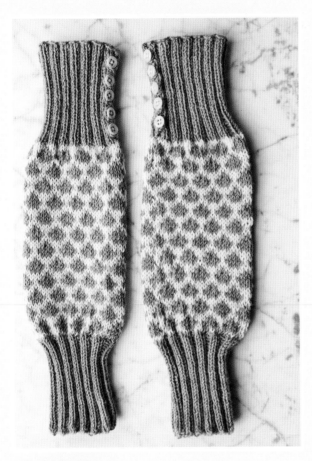

LEG WARMERS
SIZE One size

FINISHED MEASUREMENTS
Length: 15¾ in / 40 cm
Circumference at top: 9½ in / 24 cm
Circumference at ankle: 8¾ in / 22 cm

MATERIALS
Yarn: CYCA #4 (worsted/afghan/aran) Rå from Järbo Garn (100% fine Merino superwash wool; 136 yd/125 m / 50 g)

Yarn Amounts:
  MC: 50 g Natural White 23101
  CC: 100 g Brown 23105
Notions: 10 buttons about (½ in / 10 mm diameter)
Needles: U.S. sizes 6 and 7 / 4 and 4.5 mm: sets of 5 dpn
Gauge: 21 sts x 25 rows in St st on larger needles = 4 x 4 in / 10 x 10 cm.
Adjust needle sizes to obtain correct gauge if necessary.

GARMENT CONSTRUCTION AND TECHNIQUES
The leg warmers are knitted in the round on double-pointed needles, from the bottom up.

With CC and smaller size dpn, CO 48 sts. Divide sts evenly onto dpn and join; pm for beginning of end. Work around in k2, p2 ribbing for 4¼ in / 11 cm.

Change to larger size dpn and continue in St st (knit all rounds). On the first rnd, increase 12 sts evenly spaced around (= K4, M1 around) = 60 sts.

Now work following Chart A, repeating Rows 1–8 a total of 6 times.

Knit 1 rnd with MC. Cut MC; do not change needle size. With CC, work in k2, p2 ribbing for 4¼ in / 11 cm. BO in ribbing. Weave in all ends neatly on WS.

Securely sew 5 decorative buttons evenly spaced down the top ribbing.

Make the second leg warmer the same way.

Chart A

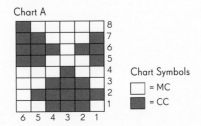

Chart Symbols
□ = MC
■ = CC

BAG

SIZE One size

FINISHED MEASUREMENTS

9½ x 6¾ in / 24 x 17 cm

MATERIALS

Yarn: CYCA #4 (worsted/afghan/aran) Rå from Järbo
   Garn (100% fine Merino superwash wool; 136
   yd/125 m / 50 g)
Yarn Amounts:
   MC: 50 g Natural White 23101
   CC: 50 g Brown 23105
Notions: felt lining fabric, 9 x 12¾ in / 23 x 32 cm
Needles: U.S. size 7 / 4.5 mm: 16 in / 40 cm circular +
   2 dpn U.S. size 6 / 4 mm for I-cord
Gauge: 21 sts x 25 rows in St st on larger needles = 4 x
   4 in / 10 x 10 cm.
Adjust needle sizes to obtain correct gauge if necessary.

GARMENT CONSTRUCTION AND TECHNIQUES

The bag is knitted around as a tube on a short circular. It
finishes with an I-cord bind-off at the top. The bottom is
then seamed and an I-cord is knit all around the edges.
The I-cord continues to form a shoulder strap. A felt lining
makes the bag sturdier and more resistant to wear and
tear.

BAG

With MC, CO 96 sts. Join, being careful not to twist
   cast-on row; pm for beg of rnd. Knit 3 rnds in St st (knit
   around).
Now work following Chart A (see page 107), repeating
   Rows 1–8 a total of 4 times and then work Rows 1–4
   once more.
Knit 2 rnds with MC and then 1 rnd with CC.

I-CORD BIND-OFF

With CC and 2 dpn U.S. size 6 / 4 mm, CO 3 sts.
Row 1: *K2, k2tog tbl. Slide the 3 sts back to left needle*. Rep * to * until 3 sts rem around top of bag. Cut
   yarn. Graft the 3 rem sts with the first 3 sts of the rnd
   with Kitchener st (see Knitting School, page 149) for an
   invisible join. Weave in all ends neatly on WS. Seam the
   bottom of the bag.

I-CORD AROUND THE BAG

With CC and 2 smaller size dpn, CO 3 sts. Slide the knitting to the right side of the needle without turning the

An I-cord is a knitted tube that looks the same all around the outside.
It's perfect for a tie, edgings, and other applications! This bag uses
three I-cord variations: a cord, a bind-off, and an edging.

work (the yarn tails will be on the left side of the work).
   K2, sl next st purlwise, yo.
Now join the cord to the bag: Beginning at the top at a
   corner of the bag, pick up and knit 1 st (as for picking
   up and knitting around a neck or other edge). Pass the
   yarnover over the knit st and then slip the slipped st over
   the knit st. Now there are 3 sts on the needle. Slide sts
   to the right side of the needle without turning.
Continue as follows: *K2, sl next st purlwise, yo. Pick up
   and knit 1 st on edge of bag. Slip the yarnover over the
   knit st. Slip the slipped st over the knit st and slide sts to
   right side of needle = 3 sts*.
Rep * to * all around the bag.
NOTE: Pick up and knit 1 st per row + an extra knit st at
   each corner.

I-CORD SHOULDER STRAP

The I-cord edging will now be worked as a loose I-cord as
   follows:
Row 1: *K3, slide sts to other end of needle; do not turn*.
   Rep * to * until cord is about 55 in / 140 cm long
Cut yarn. Graft the 3 rem sts with the first 3 sts of the rnd
   with Kitchener st (see Knitting School, page 149) for an
   invisible join. Weave in all ends neatly on WS.

FINISHING

Line the bag: Cut the felt to measure 9 x 12¾ in / 23 x
   32 cm. Fold the fabric in half and seam the sides. Insert
   the lining into the bag and sew down securely at the top
   with small invisible stitches on the inside of the I-cord
   edging.

Klara
Mittens with a "lifeline"-shaped thumb

The Klara mittens are fine and dainty—perfect for days that are cool but not cold. The sharp increase line forms a lifeline pattern at the side. The way they're constructed makes the mittens fit especially well.

SIZE One size

FINISHED MEASUREMENTS
Length: 9¾ in / 25 cm
Wrist Circumference: 8¾ in / 22 cm

MATERIALS
Yarn: CYCA #1 (fingering) Engleuld from Tusinfynd (70% wool, 30% alpaca; 252 yd/230 m / 50 g)
Yarn Amounts:
  MC: 50 g Natural White 02
  CC: 50 g Medium Blue 28
Notions: 2 stitch markers, 1 stitch holder
Needles: U.S. size 2.5 / 3 mm: set of 5 dpn
Gauge: 31 sts x 30 rows in St st pattern = 4 x 4 in / 10 x 10 cm.
Adjust needle size to obtain correct gauge if necessary.

GARMENT CONSTRUCTION AND TECHNIQUES
These mittens with richly patterned thumb gussets are worked from the bottom up.
M1R = increase 1 st to lean right (see Knitting School, page 148).
M1L = increase 1 st to lean left (see Knitting School, page 148).

LEFT MITTEN
With MC and dpn, CO 56 sts. Divide sts evenly over dpn and join; pm for beg of rnd. Knit around in St st (knit all rounds) until piece measures 3 in / 7.5 cm.

Thumb Gusset
Rnd 1: Knit until 23 sts rem; pm and complete rnd.
Rnds 2-24 (increase rnds): Work following Chart A to the marker, M1R (see Techniques above), sl m (see Knitting School, page 150), complete rnd with MC.
NOTE: The contrast color (CC) should be stranded on the WS and twisted with MC every 3-4 sts). Vary the placement of twists to avoid CC showing through to RS.
Work the increase rnd 23 times total. Work new sts into pattern.
Rnd 25: Place the previous 22 sts (= thumb sts) onto a holder or length of yarn. Knit to the marker and remove it.
Rnd 26: K2tog (= the st before and after the thumb gusset), knit the rest of the rnd following the chart = 56 sts.

Hand
**Continue knitting around following Chart A until piece measures 8¾ in / 22 cm. On the last rnd, place 2 markers: between sts 1 and 56 and between sts 28 and 29.

Chart A

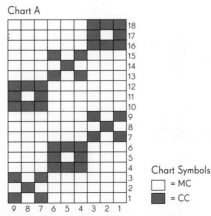

Chart Symbols
☐ = MC
■ = CC

Decrease rnd: *K1, ssk (or sl 1, k1, psso—see Knitting School, page 148). Knit until 3 sts rem before marker, k2tog, k1, sl m*; rep * to * = 52 sts.

Rep the decrease rnd 11 times = 8 sts rem.

Cut yarn and draw end through rem sts; tighten. Weave in all ends neatly on WS.

Thumb

Divide the 22 sts from holder onto 3 dpn. Knit the sts with MC and then pick up and knit 1 st on the "back," at base of thumb = 23 sts. Knit around in St st until thumb is 2 in / 5 cm long.

K2tog around until 6 sts rem. Cut yarn and draw end through rem sts; tighten. Weave in all ends neatly on WS**.

RIGHT MITTEN

With MC and dpn, CO 56 sts. Divide sts evenly over dpn and join; pm for beg of rnd. Knit around in St st (knit all rounds) until piece measures 3 in / 7.5 cm.

Thumb Gusset

Rnd 1: Knit 23; pm and complete rnd.

Rnds 2-24 (increase rnds): K23 with MC, sl m, M1L, work following Chart B to end of rnd.

Work the increase rnd 23 times total. Work new sts into pattern.

NOTE: From Rnd 3 on, the contrast color (CC) should be stranded on the WS of thumb gusset and twisted with MC every 3-4 sts. Vary the placement of twists to avoid CC showing through to RS.

Rnd 25: K23, place the previous 22 sts on a holder or length of yarn. remove marker and knit to end of rnd.

Rnd 26: Ssk (or sl 1, k1, psso—see Knitting School, page 148) with 1st st before and 1st st after thumb gusset. Knit the rest of the rnd following the chart = 56 sts.

Work from ** to ** for the rest of the mitten.

Chart B

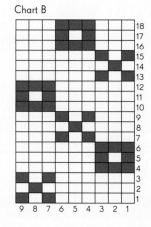

Chart Symbols
☐ = MC
■ = CC

Anna
Tam and mittens with Art-nouveau motifs

I wanted to create knitted accessories that would be just as wearable in a Värmland sheepfold as on a street in Paris. The result was Anna—a tam and mitten set that can be worn together or separately. The elegant pattern has the color of fall plums.

TAM
SIZES S/M (M/L)

FINISHED MEASUREMENTS
Head Circumference: 21¼-22 (22-22¾) in / 54-56 (56-58) cm
Tam Height: 8¾ in / 22 cm

MATERIALS
Yarn: CYCA #3 (DK/light worsted) Hverdagsuld from Tusinfynd (100% wool; 164 yd/150 m / 50 g)

Yarn Amounts:
MC: 50 (50) g Natural White 02
CC: 50 (50) g Purple 41
Needles: U.S. sizes 2.5 and 6 / 3 and 4 mm: 16 in / 40 cm circulars and, U.S. size 6 / 4 mm: set of 5 dpn
Gauge: 21 sts x 28 rows in St st on larger needles = 4 x 4 in / 10 x 10 cm.
Adjust needle sizes to obtain correct gauge if necessary.

GARMENT CONSTRUCTION AND TECHNIQUES
The tam is worked in the round on a short circular. Change to dpn when sts no longer fit around circular.

With MC and smaller size circular, CO 104 (112) sts. Join, being careful not to twist cast-on row; pm for beginning of rnd. Work around in k2, p2 ribbing for 1½ in / 4 cm.

Change to larger size circular and knit 1 rnd. Now work around in St st, following the chart, Rnds 1–24, increasing as indicated = 156 (168) sts. After completing charted rows, the rest of the tam is worked with CC only.

Rnd 25: Knit.
Rnd 26:
Size S/M: [(K5, k2tog) 11 times, k1] 2 times = 134 sts rem.
Size M/L: (K5, k2tog) around = 144 sts rem.
Rnds 27-28: Knit.
Rnd 29:
Size S/M: (K4, k2tog) 11 times, k1] 2 times = 112 sts rem.
Size M/L: (K4, K2tog) around = 120 sts rem.
Rnds 30-32: Knit.
Rnd 33:
Size S/M: (K2, k2tog, k3, k2tog) 12 times; end k2, k2tog = 87 sts rem.
Size M/L: (K2, k2tog, k3, k2tog) 13 times; end k3 = 94 sts rem.
Rnd 40: Knit.
Rnd 41: Knit, decreasing evenly spaced around to 85 (90) sts.

Rnd 42: Knit.
Rnd 43: (K3, k2tog) around = 68 (72) sts rem.
Rnd 44: Knit.
Rnd 45: (K2, k2tog) around = 51 (54) sts rem.
Rnd 46: Knit.
Rnd 47: (K1, k2tog) around = 34 (36) sts rem.
Rnd 48: K2tog around = 17 (18) sts rem.
Rnd 49: Knit.
Rnd 50: K2tog around (ending S/M with k1) = 9 sts rem.

Cut yarn; draw end through rem sts; tighten. Weave in all
ends neatly on WS.

MITTENS
SIZE One size

FINISHED MEASUREMENTS
Length of Mitten: 9 in / 23 cm

MATERIALS
Yarn: CYCA #3 (DK/light worsted) Hverdagsuld from
  Tusinfynd (100% wool; 164 yd/150 m / 50 g)
Yarn Amounts:
  MC: 50 g Natural White 02
  CC: 50 g Purple 41
Notions: 3 stitch markers
Needles: U.S. sizes 2.5 and 4 / 3 and 3.5 mm: sets of 5
  dpn
Gauge: 22 sts x 30 rows in St st on larger needles = 4 x
  4 in / 10 x 10 cm.
Adjust needle sizes to obtain correct gauge if necessary.

GARMENT CONSTRUCTION AND TECHNIQUES
The mittens are knitted in the round on double-pointed
needles.

RIGHT MITTEN
With CC and smaller size dpn, CO 48 sts. Divide sts
  evenly onto dpn and join. Work around in k2, p2 ribbing
  for 2 in / 5 cm.
Change to larger size dpn and work in St st following the
  chart.
Chart Row 17: Pm in the 2nd st of rnd (= thumb st).
Rnd 18: Begin increasing to shape thumb gusset as follows: Inc 1 st at each side of marker with a yo for each
  increase. On the next rnd, knit each yarnover through
  back loop.
Rep the increase rnd on every other rnd another 5 times =
  13 thumb gusset sts and 60 sts total.

NOTE: The increases for the thumb gusset are *not* shown
  on the chart.
After completing all the increases, place the 13 sts for
  thumb on a holder.
Next rnd: CO 1 st over the gap = 48 sts.
After completing charted rows, pm at each side (with 24
  sts between markers). Cut CC and knit 1 rnd (as well
  rest of mitten) with Natural White.
Decrease rnd: *K1, ssk (or sl 1, k1, psso—see Knitting
  School, page 148), knit until 3 sts rem before marker,
  k2tog, k1, sl m*. Rep * to * once more.
Rep the decrease rnd *every other* rnd another 5 times and
  then *every* rnd 4 times = 8 sts rem.
Cut yarn; draw end through rem sts; tighten. Weave in all
  ends neatly on WS.

Thumb
Place the 13 thumb sts on larger size dpn. With CC, knit
  the sts and pick up and knit another 3 sts on top of
  thumbhole = 16 sts total. Knit around in St st for 2½ in
  / 6 cm or desired length to tip of thumb.

Chart—Tam

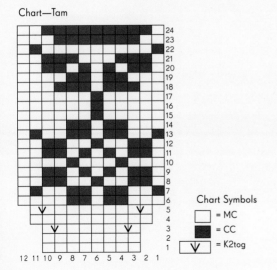

Chart Symbols

☐ = MC

■ = CC

⋁ = K2tog

Chart—Mittens

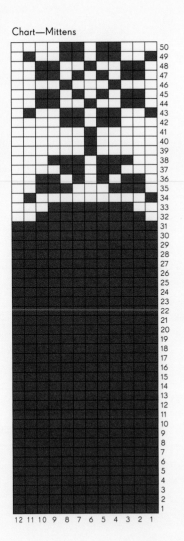

Decrease rnd: (K2tog) around = 8 sts rem.
Cut yarn and draw end through rem sts; tighten.
Weave in all ends neatly on WS.

LEFT MITTEN

Work as for right mitten but increase for the thumb gusset
on each side of the next-to-last st of the rnd (pm around
this st).

The Värmland sheep in the photos live on Gunnar
and Sara's farm at Glafsfjord in Arvika, Sweden.
The breed is a native primitive sheep breed.

Värmland sheep fleeces come in a range of colors: white, brown, gray, black, beige, and mottled.
The wool is easy to spin and felt and varies in type
from Rya (double-coated with long outer hair and
short soft wool) to Gobeläng and Finnsheep (single-
coated sheep with finer wool). Some Värmland wool
is also processed for *vadmal* (fulled wool fabric).

Sara
Knee socks with XO pattern

The Sara knee socks feature pattern panels inspired by classic blue and white porcelain. The heel is shaped with short rows, which you can learn how to work in the Knitting School on page 147. These knee socks can be paired with a lacy nightgown or worn in boots with a warm and sturdy outfit.

SIZES S/M (L/XL)

FINISHED MEASUREMENTS
Circumference at calf: 12¼ (13¾) in / 31 (35) cm to fit calf measurements 13½-14½ (15-15¾) in / 34-37 (38-40)
Foot Length: 8¾ (9, 9½, 9¾) in / 22 (23, 24, 25) cm corresponding to women's shoe sizes U.S. 4-5 (5½-6½, 7½-8½, 9½-10 ½) / Euro 34-35 (36-37, 38-39, 40-41)

MATERIALS
Yarn: CYCA #2 (sport/baby) Mellanraggi from Järbo Garn (75% superwash wool, 25% polyamide; 284 yd/260 m / 100 g)
Yarn Amounts:
   MC: 200 g Natural White 28201
   CC: 100 g Blue 28216
Notions: 2 stitch markers
Needles: U.S. sizes 1.5 and 2.5 / 2.5 and 3 mm: sets of 5 dpn
Gauge: 27 sts x 30 rnds in St st on larger needles = 4 x 4 in / 10 x 10 cm.
Adjust needle sizes to obtain correct gauge if necessary.

GARMENT CONSTRUCTION AND TECHNIQUES
The Sara knee socks are knitted in the round on double-pointed needles, from the top down. The ribbing in the cuff is twisted knit and regular purl stitches. The heel is shaped with short rows (see Knitting School, page 147). Choose the size by the cuff (two sizes given) and, when the heel is complete, the size for your foot (four sizes given).
Twisted knit stitch: Knit the stitch through the back loop.

LEG
With MC and smaller size dpn, CO 76 (86) sts. Divide sts evenly onto dpn and join. Pm for beginning of rnd. Work around in (k1tbl, p1) ribbing until cuff measures 2½ in / 6 cm.

Change to larger size dpn and knit 1 rnd, increasing as evenly spaced around as possible to 84 (96) sts. Knit 1 more rnd. Now work following Chart A, Rows 1-27 and then Rows 10-27.
Cut CC and continue with MC only. Knit around in St st until leg measures 9½ (11) in / 24 (28) cm.
Decrease Rnd: K1, ssk (or sl 1, k1, psso), knit until 3 sts rem, end with k2tog, k1.

Continue in St st and, *at the same time*, rep the decrease rnd every 4th rnd until 58 (62) sts rem. Continue until leg measures 17¾ (19¾) in / 45 (50) cm.

HEEL

Note that the heel is worked back and forth in St st over the center back 29 (31) sts. Read the instructions for short rows in the Knitting School on page 147 before you start knitting.

Row 1 (RS): Knit until 1 st rem, wrap and turn.

Row 2 (WS): Purl until 1 st rem, wrap and turn.

Row 3: Knit until 1 st rem before previous turn, wrap and turn.

Row 4: Purl until 1 st rem before previous turn, wrap and turn.

Rep Rows 3-4 until all but the center 7 sts have been wrapped.

Now the first half of the heel is complete. Up to this point, the rows became shorter and shorter. Now, on the second half of the heel, the rows become longer and longer.

Row 1: Knit until you reach the first wrapped st, knit the wrapped st (see Short Rows in the Knitting School, page 147), wrap next st and turn.

Row 2: Purl to the first wrapped st, purl the wrapped st (see Short Rows in the Knitting School, page 147), wrap next st and turn.

Row 3: Knit to the next wrapped st, lift up and knit both the wrap and the st tog, wrap the next st and turn.

Row 4: Purl to the next wrapped st, lift up and purl both the wrap and the st tog, wrap the next st and turn.

Rep Rows 3-4 until working across all the sts = 29 (31) sts on the heel.

Now work around in St st over all 58 (62) sts until the foot measures 7 (7½, 8, 8¼) in / 18 (19, 20, 21) cm, including the heel, or about 2 in / 5 cm less than total foot length. The foot length to this point depends on your chosen foot size (see sizes on previous page).

On the last rnd, divide the sts into two groups with 29 (31) sts in each = the instep and sole. Pm at each side.

TOE

Shape the toe as follows:

Decrease Rnd: *Knit until 2 sts before marker, ssk (or sl 1, k1, psso—see Knitting School, page 150), sl m, k2tog*; rep * to * once more.

Rep the decrease rnd on every other rnd 6 (7) times and then on every rnd until 10 sts rem. Cut yarn and draw end through rem sts; tighten. Weave in all ends neatly on WS.

Make the second sock the same way.

Chart A

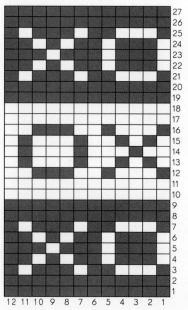

Chart Symbols

☐ = MC

■ = CC

VARIATION ON A THEME

The knee socks in this photo are a variation of the Sara Knee socks and are a good example of how different patterns from the Pattern Library at the end of the book can be combined for a new look. When you combine several motifs in new ways, it's almost as good as a monogram!

If you want to knit this version of the socks, you need to make the following changes:

Knit the leg in size S/M if you want a similar placement of the pattern bands.

Work the ribbing as k2, p2 instead of the twisted rib as given in the original pattern. After the ribbing, knit 3 rnds with MC.

Substitute a rose panel (see page 144) for the XO motif, but work 2 white sts at the beginning and end of the rnd so the rose panel will fit evenly around. Next, work Dala Pattern C (see page 139), part of Nordic Panel B (see page 141) with 1 st between each snowflake and finish with Öland Pattern D (see page 139).

NOTE: Knit 3 rnds with MC between each pattern panel.

Begin the leg shaping as soon as the pattern panels are finished. This stocking will be about 1¼ in / 3 cm longer than the original version of Sara.

Elnaz
Persian slippers with star motifs

These slippers are worked from the toe up and are the result of a meeting between a Persian slipper model, the classic eight-petaled rose, and Swedish ragg socks. Elnaz is one of the photo models in the book and her name means "the finest generation".

SIZES Women's U.S. shoe size 7½-9½ / Euro 38-40

FINISHED MEASUREMENTS
Foot Length: 9¾ in / 25 cm

MATERIALS
Yarn: CYCA #4 (worsted/afghan/aran) Raggi from Järbo Garn (70% wool, 30% polyamide; 165 yd/151 m / 100 g)
Yarn Amounts:
  MC: 100 g Petroleum 15123
  CC: 100 g Natural White 1500
Needles: U.S. sizes 6 and 7 / 4 and 4.5 mm: sets of 5 dpn
Gauge: 18-19 sts x 24 rows in St st on larger needles = 4 x 4 in / 10 x 10 cm.
Adjust needle sizes to obtain correct gauge if necessary.

SLIPPERS
With MC and 2 larger size dpn held together, CO 11 sts.

Carefully remove 1 dpn and then pick up and knit 9 sts along the other side of the cast-on edge. Divide the sts onto 4 dpn: 6 sts on Needle 1, 5 sts on Needle 2, 5 sts on Needle 3, and 4 sts on Needle 4 = 22 sts total. Join to work in the round.
Rnd 1: K1, yo, k9, yo, k1, yo, k9, yo = 24 sts. On following rnds, knit yarnover through back loop.
Rnds 2, 4, 6, and 8: K1, k1tbl (into yarnover), knit to next yarnover, k1tbl, k1, k1tbl, knit to next yarnover, k1tbl.
Rnd 3: K1, yo, k11, yo, k1, yo, k11, yo = 28 sts.
Rnd 5: K1, yo, k13, yo, k1, yo, k13, yo = 32 sts.
Rnd 7: K1, yo, k15, yo, k1, yo, k15, yo = 36 sts.
Rnd 9: K1, yo, k17, yo, k1, yo, k17, yo = 40 sts.
Rnd 10: Work as for Rnd 2.
Now work following Chart A. After completing charted rows, change to CC and smaller size dpn. Knit 4 rows back and forth over the sts on the first two dpn. BO these sts.
With CC: CO 21 new sts. Knit 3 rows back and forth. These new sts correspond to those previously on the first two needles. Go back to knitting in the round and work following Chart B. BO.

FINISHING
Graft the sts of the heel inside the bound-off edge.
Seam the garter stitch side edges: Place edge over edge and sew through both layers. Weave in all ends neatly on WS. Make the second slipper the same way.

Chart A

Chart B

Chart Symbols

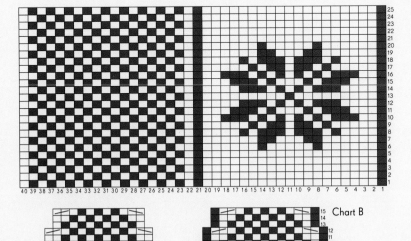

= k2tog tbl
= k2tog
= MC
= CC

PATTERN LIBRARY

The pattern library is divided into three sections:

◊ Stars, flowers, animals, and people
◊ Landscape motifs
◊ Borders and panels

◊ The patterns are taken from my collection of knitting magazines (from the 1940s onwards), newspaper clippings, and notes and loose pattern sheets, as well as old knitted garments. At the end of each pattern, you'll find a few lines about their background and history.

◊ All the patterns are shown as both a knitted swatch and a chart. The swatches provide a clear picture of how the pattern can look when it has been knitted, and the chart shows how the pattern is constructed.

◊ The pattern repeat (which is given at the end of each pattern) indicates how many stitches and rows the pattern is a multiple of. These details are important to know if you want to substitute the pattern for one of those in a garment in the book or when you create your own garments. Patterns with the same multiples for a stitch count are interchangeable with each other.

◊ Take into consideration that different color combinations can produce different results. If you are uncertain about color choices, you should either knit a swatch or sketch out various options on a copy of the pattern graph on page 156.

◊ For the patterns to be clear, it is important that colors have a sufficient contrast. A good way to check this is to photograph the yarn skein with a cell phone camera and then view it through the black-white filter. That will make it obvious if the color's gray tones contrast enough. If they don't, you should consider some other options.

◊ If the stitch count of the pattern you want to use on a certain garment doesn't work evenly into the total stitch count, it is sometimes possible to adjust the stitch repeats by, for example, increasing or decreasing the number of stitches between each pattern element. If that doesn't work, you can adjust the stitch count of the garment, as long as it doesn't affect the size of the garment. One common way for adjusting the patterns is to convert an even-numbered repeat to an odd-numbered one, or vice versa. Some patterns need an odd-numbered stitch count so the motif can be centered while others need an even stitch count so it repeats regularly.

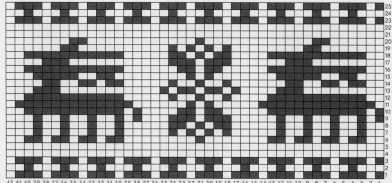

REINDEER

The reindeer is a well-loved motif in the knitting world—and in both Sweden and Norway. In this pattern, the reindeer are elements of a pretty panel. (See how the pattern is repeated on the Sigrid sweater, page 58.) It's exciting to experiment with figurative motifs such as this one! By changing the direction the reindeer face, you can produce various effects. For example, it can be very effective to have the animals facing each other as on the Sigrid sweater; or you can add movement and balance to a garment by repeating the reindeer panel lengthwise, with the reindeer facing right in the first repetition, then left in the second repetition, and right again in the third repetition, etc.

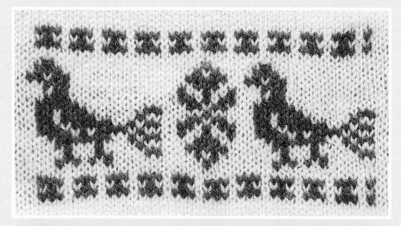

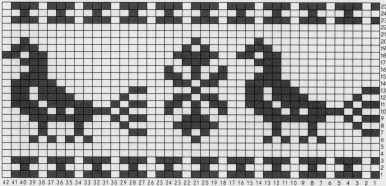

BIRDS

This playful panel features generic birds. Birds, just like hearts, roses, and stars, are an often-repeated motif in Swedish knitting traditions. (See how the pattern is repeated on page 58.) Play with the direction the birds face as described above in the paragraph about reindeer—it adds life and movement to the motif. Why not choose a single bird out of a pattern and incorporate it into, for example, a mitten or hat, or as a discreet embellishment for a sleeve?

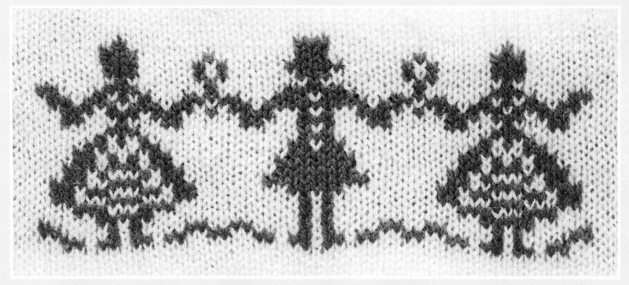

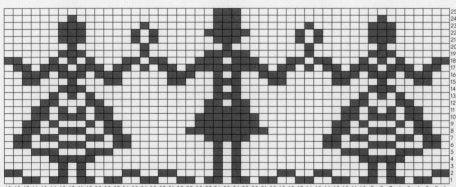

PEOPLE
— HAND IN HAND

There are many variations of this folkloric pattern, with men and women side by side and hand in hand. This particular one, originally from the early twentieth century, was taken from a child's knitted dress. The pattern repeat is 49 stitches x 25 rows.

ROUND FLOWERS

This pattern was taken from a hat. The flowers combine with lice to produce a dense, flowing two-color pattern.
The pattern repeat is 28 stitches x 36 rows.

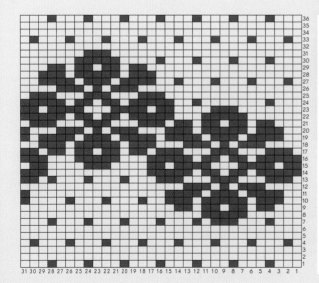

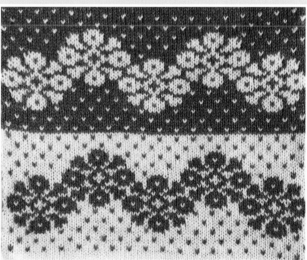

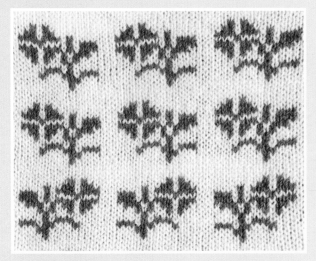

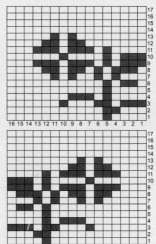

FLOWERS

Sweet flowers gathered from a lice sweater pattern in an undated daily paper. The motif can be mirror-imaged as shown on the sample swatch.
The pattern repeat is 16 stitches x 17 rows.

CROWNS

A royal symbol transformed into a knitting pattern. The crown, which is also a classic motif for marking textiles, can be repeated for a well-balanced pattern as shown here. The pattern repeat is 18 stitches x 22 rows.

EIGHT-PETALED ROSES

The eight-petaled rose is a timeless pattern found in every corner of the world. I've combined it with tiny stars here. The pattern repeat is 24 stitches x 36 rows.

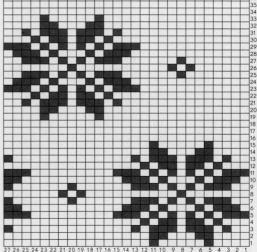

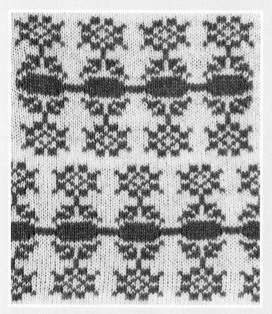

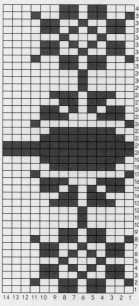

ART NOUVEAU ROSES

These flowers from the 1940s were influenced by Art Nouveau style. The pattern makes a fine finish or beginning in a primarily single-color section—exactly as shown in the Anna tam and mitten set (see page 114).

The pattern repeat is 12 stitches x 20 rows.

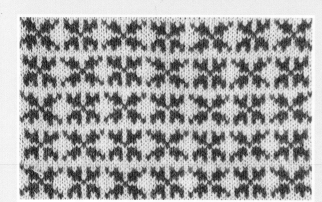

SMALL STARS

These small stars or flowers, forming an enchanting all-over pattern, were found charted in a pattern notebook.

The pattern repeat is 18 stitches x 8 rows.

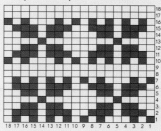

CANDLE FLOWERS

These stylized flowers came from a knitting magazine published in 1945. The colors used for the swatch are the same as in the original.

The pattern repeat is 22 stitches x 34 rows.

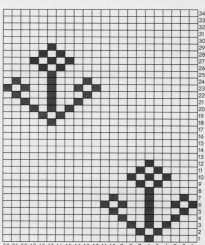

SQUIRRELS AND EIGHT-PETALED ROSES

Eight-petaled roses combine with sweet little squirrels for a fanciful overall pattern. The original motif covered a boy's pullover. The published pattern was found on an old torn-out newspaper page.

The pattern repeat is 32 stitches x 48 rows.

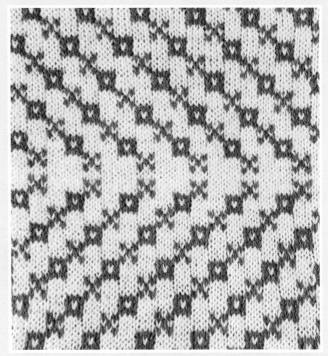

FLORAL VINES

A simple geometric pattern similar to floral vines. From a notepaper in a pattern notebook. The pattern repeat is 9 stitches x 18 rows.

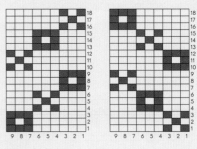

VÄSTMANLAND A

X and O patterns are common in the Fair Isle tradition. It was referred to as a Västmanland pattern in a 1947 Swedish knitting magazine. It becomes especially charming considering that X and O means "hugs and kisses" in today's internet terminology. The pattern repeat is 12 stitches x 18 rows.

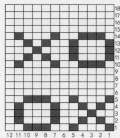

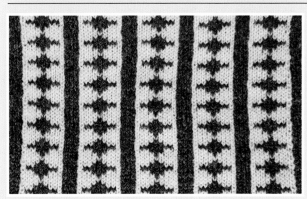

ÖLAND A

The Swedish island of Öland has a strong knitting tradition and a rich pattern treasury—especially when it comes to mittens. Here's a geometric pattern that was originally worked in brown on a white background.
The pattern repeat is 12 stitches x 6 rows.

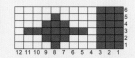

VÄSTMANLAND B

These fine harlequin motifs originally embellished a sports sweater. The pattern was published in a 1940s knitting magazine.
The pattern repeat is 16 stitches x 37 rows.

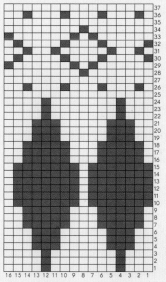

ÖLAND B

A variation on the classic "goose eye" weaving pattern and a good example of how weaving patterns can be adapted for knitting.

The pattern repeat is 6 stitches x 6 rows.

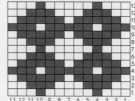

VÄSTMANLAND C

This motif enhanced the shoulders of a vintage cardigan for men. In the original garment, the motifs are white against a brown background.

The pattern repeat is 6 stitches x 26 rows.

VÄSTMANLAND D

A pretty sweater pattern originally knitted in brown on a gray background. The pattern has closely-spaced color changes which make it an easy-to-knit two-color pattern.

The pattern repeat is 8 stitches x 8 rows.

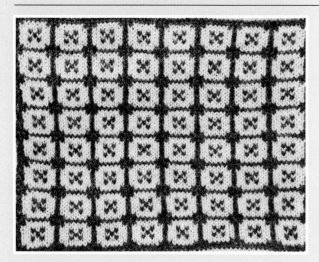

HÄLSINGLAND

An eight-petaled rose combined with a flower basket—a pattern very like those found in old books of textile marking patterns. This is a clear example of how a motif from other textile techniques, such as embroidery, can be adapted for knitting. The square blocking of the motifs makes it an inviting choice for a sweater pocket, blanket square, or even a bag.

The pattern repeat is 62 stitches x 67 rows.

GÄSTRIKLAND A

This droplet pattern is knitted here as in the original, red on a gray background. It's fun to vary color combinations for two-color designs such as this one. The two colors will be perceived very differently depending on which is the background color and which is the pattern color. Try it out by knitting a sample swatch, choosing two colors with high contrast values. Knit a few repeats and then switch the background and pattern colors. Now you can choose the variation you like best!

The pattern repeat is 6 stitches x 8 rows.

GÄSTRIKLAND B

Closely-spaced two-color motifs that will look great on mittens. Originally, these small blocked "flowers" were knitted in blue against a white background and surrounded by a red frame.

The pattern repeat is 6 stitches x 7 rows.

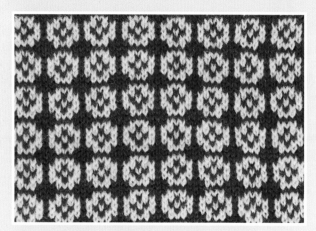

GOTLAND

Flowers lined up in a row make a pretty panel. I found this pattern on a mitten knitted by an old woman who lived on the Swedish island of Gotland but it was also featured in a 1940s knitting magazine.

The pattern repeat is 12 stitches x 35 rows.

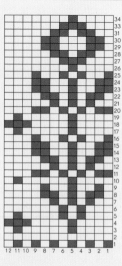

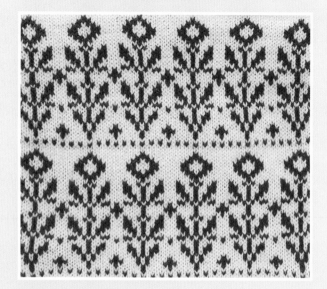

ÖLAND C

A classic Öland pattern with flowers and windmills.

The pattern repeat is 22 stitches x 32 rows.

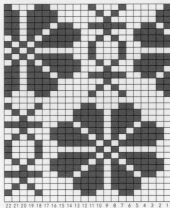

HALLAND

This classic pattern from the Swedish province of Halland is a regular feature on vintage sweaters and cardigans.

The pattern repeat is 30 stitches x 74 rows.

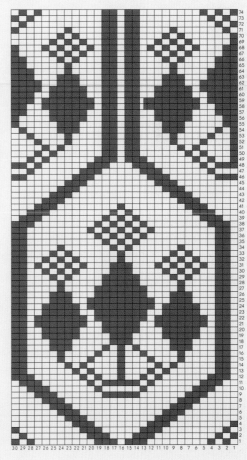

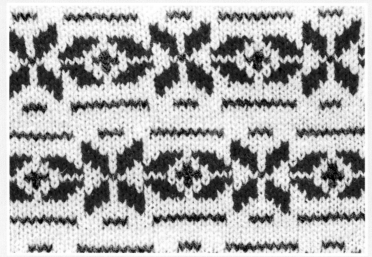

DALARNA A

Small panels from a cardigan knitted in Dalarna sometime in the 1930s by a woman named Kristin. The pattern was originally worked in five colors, as on the Kristin cardigan shown on page 80.
The pattern repeat is 18 stitches x 15 rows.

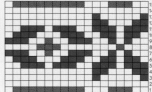

DALARNA B

A wide panel from a cardigan knitted by a woman named Kristin in Dalarna sometime in the 1930s.
The pattern repeat is 18 stitches x 33 rows.

In a little piece of writing titled "The Village of My Childhood," my father's maternal grandfather, John Hansson, describes life in the village of Nyberget in Västmanland at the beginning of the twentieth century. Among other things, we learn how wool was handled by the women of the village and what they knitted with it.

"Almost everyone in the village had some sheep. They were shorn by the women and the wool was used primarily for mittens and socks. The wool was first carded into round, soft rolls called rolags, and was eventually spun into yarn of various thicknesses, depending on what the finished yarn would be used for. Afterwards, the yarn was knitted into long, warm, all-wool stockings and even the women wore them, at least for everyday wear."

On page 119, you can find a description of my interpretation of these long wool stockings. You can also use the description as the starting point for your own pattern mix—exactly as I did when I knitted my variation on the Sara knee socks. Read more about this on page 122.

BLEKINGE

Sweet stripes with tiny flowers originally knitted in green and beige. This pattern is an excellent frame for larger and more detailed motifs. This type of complementary pattern is good for collecting.
The pattern repeat is 4 stitches x 10 rows.

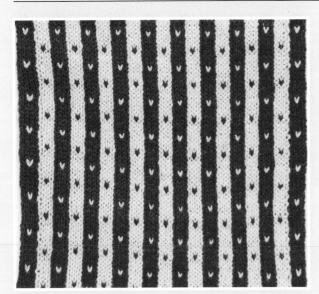

ÖLAND D

This Öland pattern was published in a knitting magazine in 1946. It is similar to the Norwegian Fana pattern but it has vertical stripes instead of horizontal ones. It's also part of the Bohus knitting pattern archive under the name "Running Stripe," designed by Emma Jacobsson in 1947.
The pattern repeat is 6 stitches x 8 rows.

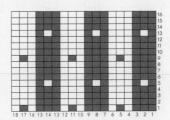

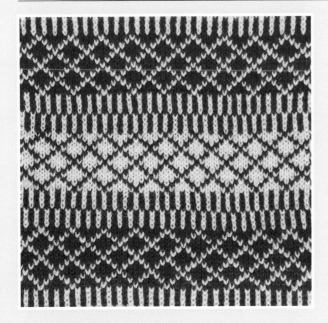

DALARNA C

An elegant pattern and a personal favorite, taken from a Dala sweater featured in a 1940s knitting magazine. The closely-spaced color changes and the geometric structure make this pattern easy to knit and to memorize—but it looks splendid and advanced! This pattern also invites exciting color combinations because it can be knitted so that each pattern section is worked in two distinct color combinations. (See the Johanna wrist warmers on page 99.)
The pattern repeat is 6 stitches x 21 rows.

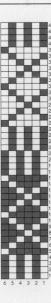

SNOWFLAKES

I found this beautiful panel in an old notebook of knitting patterns. I think it looks like snowflakes. The panel will be a lovely eye-catcher when placed alone on the lower edge of a sweater, or on sock cuffs. On page 62, you can see how the panel embellishes the sleeves on the Kajsa dress.

When it comes to detail-rich patterns such as this one, it's important to choose colors that stand in stark contrast to each other—that way the pattern will display at its best. If you're uncertain about color choices, it's a good idea to sketch the motifs with the help of the blank graph paper on page 156, or use the "photo method" described on page 127. The pattern repeat is 48 stitches x 37 rows.

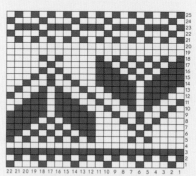

WINTER FLOWERS

This pretty flower panel appeared on a child's ski pullover from 1947. It was originally knitted in white on a red background.
The pattern repeat is 22 stitches x 25 rows.

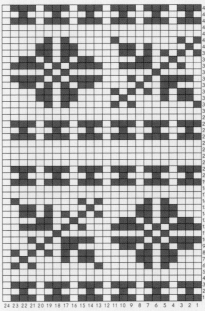

NORDIC PANEL A

Flowers and stylized snowflakes. One of several panels on a Nordic ski sweater from the 1940s. The pattern repeat is 24 stitches x 46 rows.

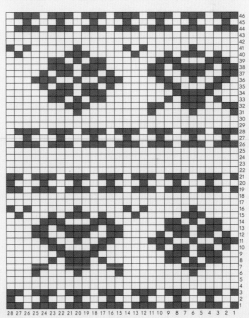

NORDIC PANEL B

A classic panel from a Nordic ski sweater with roots in the 1940s. The pattern repeat is 28 stitches x 46 rows.

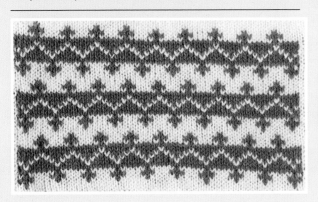

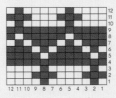

DIAGONAL STRIPES

This fanciful stripe variation was originally knitted in white against a gray background. The zigzag panel changed colors between green, red, and brown.
The pattern repeat is 12 stitches x 12 rows.

STAR PANEL

This pretty panel is composed of eight-pointed stars (i.e., eight-petaled roses). It is common to have a large main motif such as the one shown here, composed from smaller elements that partly make the pattern more elegant and partly emphasize the two-color knitting because the distance between the color changes is shorter. When it comes to pattern knitting, form and function often go hand in hand, and a pattern that's easy to knit is also especially full of life. Small secondary motifs are also important for making the pattern function as a whole. More examples of how the eight-pointed star is framed and embellished can be found on pages 130 (Eight-petaled Rose), 132 (Squirrels and Eight-petaled Roses), and 135 (Hälsingland). The pattern repeat is 26 stitches x 29 rows.

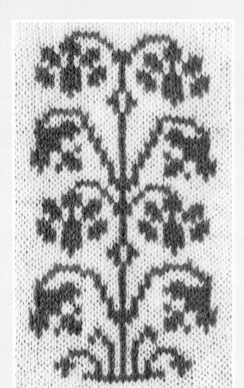

GROWING FLOWERS

A luxurious pattern from a sports sweater with roots in the 1940s. In the original, the flowers were knitted in gray against a white background. The pattern repeat is 29 stitches x 57 rows.

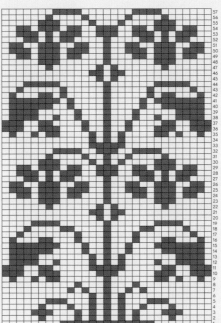

COLUMNS

This panel from the 1940s will remind you of ancient columns. It's exciting to see how the impression of the pattern changes when you shift the pattern and background colors.
The pattern repeat is 8 stitches x 44 rows.

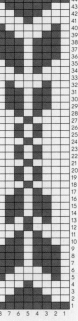

ARABESQUE HEARTS

Braided hearts produce panels. The arabesque hearts originally embellished a cardigan from a 1946 knitting magazine. The panel can be used singly or repeated over the entire surface. It's also effective to let the lines of hearts change directions, as on this sample swatch!
The pattern repeat is 11 stitches x 10 rows.

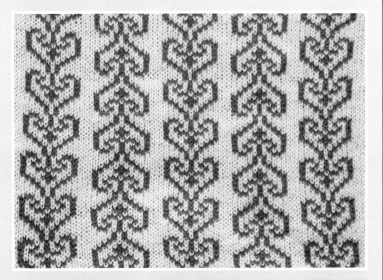

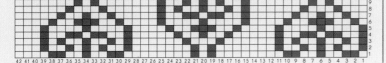

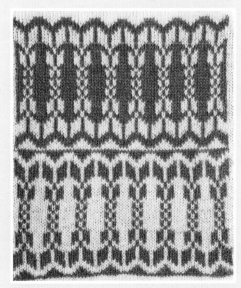

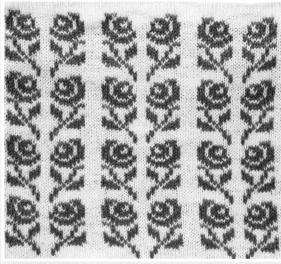

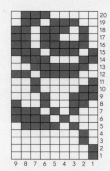
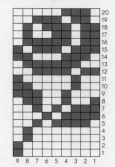

ROSE PANELS

During the 1940s, this type of rose panel was the height of fashion. Seen historically, the roses were commonly used as motifs for knitted goods—not least on mittens. The roses in the panel can be used as a set where two roses with respective right- and left- facing are combined, or one and one as on the Rose cardigan (see page 52), where a "vine" on each button band decorates the front. It's also fine to let the panel frame a corner, because it can be knitted vertically or horizontally. For example, a panel like this can work very well as a decoration on a baby blanket. Of course, it's also good to repeat the roses over a large surface, as in these sample swatches.

The pattern repeat for vertical roses is 9 stitches x 20 rows; for horizontal roses, 20 stitches x 9 rows.

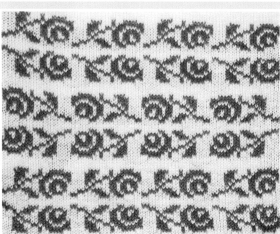

PANEL OF WISHES

The panel with the poetic name is taken from a 1940s knitting magazine. It decorated the front and sleeves of a cardigan, but originally came from an old mitten. The panel can either function alone (by placing it inside the front edges of a cardigan, for example)—or be repeated over an entire surface, as on the sample swatch.

The pattern repeat is 31 stitches x 20 rows.

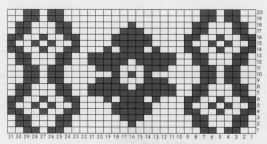

ABBREVIATIONS

ABBREVIATIONS

beg	begin(s)(ning)	psso	pass slipped stitch over
BO	bind off (British = cast off)	rem	remain(ing)(s)
CC	contrast color (also called a pattern color)	rep	repeat(s)
cm	centimeter(s)	RLI	right lifted increase = insert needle into right side of stitch below needle and knit into it; knit stitch on needle = 1 stitch increased (see page 148)
CO	cast on		
dec	decrease(s)		
est	established (i.e., work as set up)		
in	inch(es)	RS	right side
inc	increase(s)	sk2p	sl 1, k2tog, psso = 2 stitches decreased
k	knit	sl	slip
k2tog	knit 2 stitches together = 1 stitch decreased; right-leaning decrease	sl m	slip marker
		ssk	(slip 1 st knitwise) 2 times; knit the stitches together through back loops = 1 stitch decreased; left-leaning decrease
M1	make 1 = lift strand between 2 sts and knit into back loop		
M1L	make 1 left (see page 148)	st(s)	stitch(es)
M1R	make 1 right (see page 148)	St st	stockinette stitch (British = stocking stitch)
MC	main color (also called a background color)	WS	wrong side
mm	millimeters	wyb	with yarn held in back
p	purl	wyf	with yarn held in front
p2tog	purl 2 stitches together = 1 stitch decreased	yd	yard(s)
pm	place marker	yo	yarnover

KNITTING SCHOOL

TWO-COLOR STRANDED KNITTING

Knitting patterns with two or more colors worked at the same time are common in Swedish and Nordic knitting traditions. The technique produces a firm and warming structure because the yarn strands are doubled or tripled as you knit.

There are various ways to hold the yarn when knitting two-color stranded knitting. In Sweden, it's most common to hold the yarn in the left hand—one strand over the index finger and the other over the middle finger. The yarn from the ball is then gathered in the hand and held with the ring and little fingers. However, there are other ways to hold the yarn. For example, I hold one strand over the thumb and the other over my index finger. Try out various methods and find out what works best for you. It's most important that you hold the strands with even tension so the yarn that is "floating" doesn't pull in on the wrong side.

When knitting patterns with two colors, one color is thought of as the pattern or contrast color (CC), which will dominate. The other is the background or main color (MC), which recedes into the background. The strands should be held so that the contrast color is nearest the knitting and always comes from underneath. That way, the pattern color will dominate and be seen more clearly against the background color. In contrast, the main or background color is held further away from the knitted fabric and comes from above. It is important to be consistent with the order of the colors, because otherwise the pattern may look rippled or "smudgy."

When you are knitting with one color, the other color "floats" on the wrong side of the work. The yarn on the wrong side should have the same tension as for the rest of the work; if it doesn't, the fabric will be puckered (if you draw in too much) or floppy (if you draw in too little).

If you're knitting more than three or four stitches in the same color, it's a good idea to twist the strand floating on the wrong side around the working yarn. That way you'll avoid long strands, which will catch a lot when you put on the garment. But don't twist the yarns in the same place on each row or round—if you do, the floating strand will be visible on the right side. Always shift the twists so they don't stack up.

In order for your two-color stranded knitting to look its best, it's important that you:

◊ maintain as even a tension as possible
◊ make sure the yarn floating on the wrong side has enough slack
◊ hold the main and contrast colors in the correct order
◊ twist the strands around each other whenever there are more than 3 or 4 stitches with the same color
◊ do not stack the twists on the wrong side

SHORT ROWS

Knitting short rows means that you knit only part of a row or round. In order to avoid holes when turning, stitches are wrapped at the turn. Here's how to wrap a stitch:

On the RS: Bring the yarn to the front of the work, slip the next stitch purlwise to the right needle. Bring yarn to back of work and slip the stitch back to the left needle. Turn the work.

When you are going to knit a wrapped stitch, insert the needle through both the stitch and the wrap and knit together.

On the WS: With the yarn in back of the work, slip the next stitch purlwise to the right needle. Bring the yarn to the front of the work and slip the stitch back to the left needle. Turn the work.

When you are going to purl a wrapped stitch, insert the needle through both the stitch and the wrap and purl together.

DECREASES

Knit 2 stitches together (k2tog)—right-leaning decrease

Insert needle knitwise into second stitch and then first st on left needle and then knit the stitches together.

Slip 1—knit 1—pass slipped stitch over (sl 1, k1, psso)—left-leaning decrease

Slip 1 stitch knitwise from left to right needle, knit 1, and then pass the slipped stitch over the knitted one. This can be substituted with ssk (see Abbreviations on page 146).

Double decrease (sk2p)

Slip 1 stitch knitwise from left to right needle, knit 2tog, and then pass the slipped stitch over the k2tog.

INCREASES

Invisible increases are useful when you are knitting cardigans or pullovers from the top down. Here are three options:

Invisible left-leaning increase (M1L)

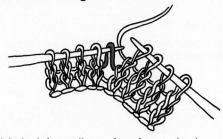

1. With the left needle tip, from front to back, pick up the strand between two stitches and lift onto left needle.

2. Knit 1 through the back loop as shown by the arrow.

3. A new stitch that leans to the left has been formed.

Invisible right-leaning increase (M1R)

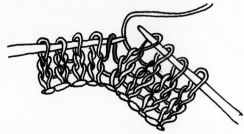

1. With the left needle tip, from back to front, pick up the strand between two stitches and lift onto left needle.

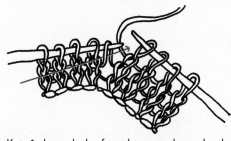

2. Knit 1 through the front loop as shown by the arrow.

3. A new stitch that leans to the right has been formed.

Invisible increase in stitch below—right-lifted increase (RLI)

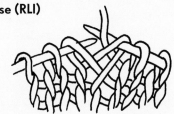

1. Insert the right needle tip into the right side of the stitch loop of the stitch below the one on the left needle. Pick up the loop and place on left needle. Knit into the loop.

2. Knit 1 into the original stitch on the left needle.

EMBROIDERING WITH DUPLICATE STITCH

Duplicate stitch embroidery (also called Swiss darning) imitates the knit stitch and can be used as an alternative to pattern knitting. The technique is especially good for small motifs or small parts of a larger knitted motif.

Duplicate stitch embroidery is also useful when you are refreshing an old garment. Maybe you are knitting a child's sweater that will later be passed on to another relative? It's entirely practical to embroider a name or embellishment, so you can rip it out later and embroider something new for the new recipient of the garment.

Duplicate stitch is also perfect for correcting little mistakes in a knitted color pattern!

Here's how: Use a blunt-tipped tapestry needle. Either embroider with yarn the same thickness as the knitting yarn or a slightly thicker yarn; a thinner yarn won't cover the stitches.

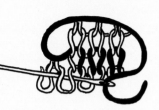 

GRAFTING WITH DUPLICATE STITCH = KITCHENER STITCH

When joining two knitted pieces with live stitches, you can sew them together with Kitchener stitch to make an invisible seam. The new stitches will "melt" into the structure without a splice becoming visible. This technique is used, for example, on the Maja cowl on page 105.

Holding the two sets of stitches parallel:

1. Insert tapestry needle knitwise into first stitch on front knitting needle and slip the stitch off the needle.

2. Insert needle purlwise into next st on front needle but do not slip stitch off knitting needle.

3. Insert needle purlwise into first st on back needle and slip stitch off the needle.

4. Insert needle knitwise into next stitch on back needle but do not slip stitch off needle.

Repeat these steps until all stitches have been joined.

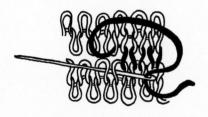

Here's an example of duplicate stitch embroidery.

CROCHETED PROVISIONAL CAST-ON

Sometimes you need to have access to live stitches on both sides of the cast-on. In that case, you can begin with a provisional cast-on that will later be removed to release the stitches. One method to do this is a crocheted provisional cast-on. Unless otherwise specified, use a smooth contrast color waste yarn for the cast-on.

1. Make a slip knot and place the loop over a crochet hook. Place the hook perpendicular to the knitting needle and lay the yarn end (from the ball) behind the knitting needle.

2. With the yarn behind the needle: move the hook over the needle and catch the yarn.

3. Draw the yarn through the loop on the hook as for a slip stitch.

4. Repeat 2 and 3 until you have the desired number of stitches on the knitting needle.

5. End with a couple of chain stitches. Cut yarn and draw end through last chain stitch. When it comes time to release the stitches, undo the chain stitches and then release the stitches by carefully removing the waste yarn. It's best to work stitch by stitch, placing each released stitch onto the knitting needle.

REINFORCING BUTTONHOLES

To help knitted buttonholes maintain their shape and avoid wear, you can reinforce them. This means that you surround the buttonhole with buttonhole stitch.

Here's how: With a blunt-tipped wool embroidery needle, begin by surrounding the buttonhole with running stitch. Next, work around the hole with very closely-spaced buttonhole stitch (see drawing below).

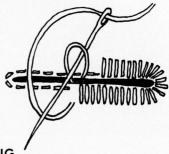

WET BLOCKING

Before seaming a knitted garment or finishing a seamless piece, you'll get the best results if you first wet block the garment. The process will even out any inconsistencies because the fibers will relax so the stitches can align properly.

Begin by carefully submerging the garment into lukewarm water. Gently squeeze out excess water (or roll in a towel) and then pat the pieces out to finished measurements on a blocking mat or ironing board. Pin out the pieces and leave overnight to dry. Alternately, you can pat out the pieces to finished measurements, spritz with water until damp or cover with a damp towel. Leave overnight to dry.

SLIPPING MARKERS

Stitch markers, either plastic or metal rings, are very useful. Place them (pm = place marker) between two stitches to help you keep your place in the knitting (for example, to mark off pattern repeats). To slip the marker (sl m), means that you simply slide the marker from the left to the right needle.

THAT LITTLE SOMETHING EXTRA

◇ Do you want to give away a knitted cardigan? It's a nice idea to sew an extra button on the inside of the band so the recipient will have one in reserve in case a button is lost.
◇ Do you want to give away a knitted garment? Make a little yarn butterfly with any leftovers. Put the butterfly plus a blunt-tipped tapestry needle in a little bag to give to the recipient with the sweater. That way, the person can darn the garment with the same yarn if need be.

YARN SOURCES

Istex: www.istex.is/english (distributed in the U.S. by www.berroco.com)

Järbo Garn: www.jarbo.se
Gästrike 2-ply
Gästrike 4-ply
Mellanraggi
Rå
Ulla

Rauma Garn: www.raumaull.no (distributed in the U.S. by www.theyarnguys.com)
Finullgarn

Sandnes Garn: www.sandnesgarn.no or sandnes-garn.com
Alpakka Ull (Alpaca Wool)
Suri Alpacka
Tove

Tusindfynd CPH: www.tusinfyndcph.dk
Engleuld (angel wool)
Hverdagsuld (everyday wool)

If you are unable to obtain any of the yarn used in this book, it can be replaced with a yarn of a similar weight and composition. Please note, however, the finished projects may vary slightly from those shown, depending on the yarn used. Try www.yarnsub.com for suggestions.

For more information on selecting or substituting yarn, contact your local yarn shop or an online store; they are familiar with all types of yarns and would be happy to help you. Additionally, the online knitting community at Ravelry.com has forums where you can post questions about specific yarns. Yarns come and go so quickly these days and there are so many beautiful yarns available.

ACKNOWLEDGMENTS

Maja would like to thank

Maria—because you took the photos with such a sensitive eye and steady hand, and because you shared with me your pleasure in your work and richness of ideas.

Katy—for the lovely form, lively illustrations and a style-conscious way of working.

Alexandra—because you believed in me and my book—and for your infectious enthusiasm, smart points of view, and careful guidance.

Annika—for steadying help, good guidance, and an unperturbable calm. Everything that was troublesome become so much easier when you showed me the way.

Linda—for your precise work with the charts and for support through thick and thin. There's no way to express how much your supportive ideas and our exchanges meant to me.

Kalle—for constant back-up and support—the quickly-sent packages of yarn and small indispensable reminders of what it all really means. The heart on the sweater 4-ever!

Kristina—(and all the other good friends at Järbo Garn)—for showing belief and invaluable encouragement.

Linnéa—for your fantastic job with the sample swatches! Seldom has working together functioned so seamlessly. It was a pure pleasure to have you helping with this.

Kerstin—for the pretty braids and hair styling, friendship, and everything so valuable that you shared.

Sara Ö and Sandra S—because you always such a good sounding board when I needed it, and for your wise suggestions when it came to the pattern texts and construction.

Anna B—for invaluable support and caring through the years.

Carin F—because you supported me in a special way when I really needed it and for your unreserved faith in my powers of creation!

Instagram friends, blog readers, and handcraft colleagues—for warmth, encouragement, and a supportive inspiration! What a wonderful yarn world we share!

Friends and relatives—because you gave my life goals and meaning.

Fredrika—for a friendship through everything. Also, for the laughter, understanding, and support—which was always there when I most needed it.

Pappa Johnny and Mamma Kajsa, the best ever parents—because you are my foremost supporters, the most important role models, and most beloved colleagues. And because you taught me to think freely and courageously, and to go my own way! Long live the Karlsson family and art work!

Lisa—because you are the world's best and most beloved sister, and my eternally secure harbor!

Daniel—because you always believed in me, always supported me, and so generously helped me with everything and more. And for all the valuable tips and conversations. No book without you—I want you to know that!

Elsa and Johanna—because you are the wonderful girls you are, and for everything we share.

Greta—because I got to be your mother! Your happy creativity, imagination, and dexterity inspire me every day.

Thank you to all the wonderful models!
Anna Karlsson
Clara Rosenlöf
Elnaz Baghlanian
Karin Lidén
Kristin Päevä
Zandra Lidén

Thank you to the dexterous knitters
Sandra Stenqvist (Anna, Hulda, Kerstin and Rosa)
Kajsa Vuorela (Kajsa and Sigrid)
Sara Öhman (Sara)
Evelina Berg (Maja)
Ulrica Loeb (Fredrika)
All other garments knitted by Maja

All of the charts in the book were drawn by Linda Brodin.

The sample swatches in the Pattern Library were machine-knit by Linnéa Öhman.

Hair styling for photography of the garments Klara, Kajsa, Anna, Maja, and Esther: Kerstin Ekling.

Photo sites, thank you to:
BarCentral www.barcentral.se)
Christoffer's Flowers, Stockholm
Rackstad Museum and Oppstuhage (www.rackstadmuseet.se)
Tyresö Castle (www.nordiskamuseet.se/tyreso-slott)
Gunnar Micholds and Sara Boudiaf's Värmlandsgård at Glafsfjord. With special thanks for letting us borrow the sheep and hens!

PATTERN GRAPH TEMPLATE

Here's a template for you to use for combining different motifs from the Pattern Library into your own designs or to try out various color combinations. You can also find out what happens if you change the direction of certain patterns, or adapt some of the patterns by making small changes. Perhaps you want to create a completely new pattern by combining small elements from several of the motifs in the library? That's how I created the pattern for the Flora arm warmers (see page 97).

How you want to use the pattern graph template is up to you—only your imagination sets the limits! Try sketching with color pencils of the type used for coloring books—you can usually find them in many colors. Copy this book page before you begin drawing so that you can work with the template as many times as you want!

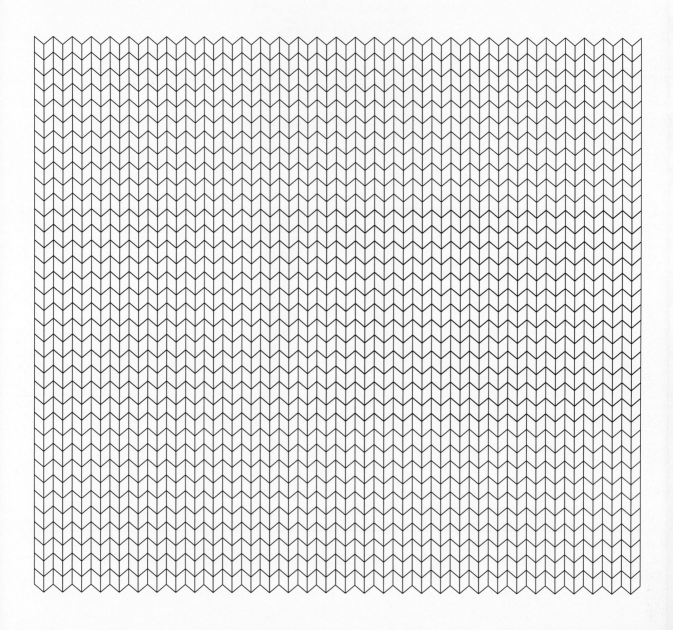

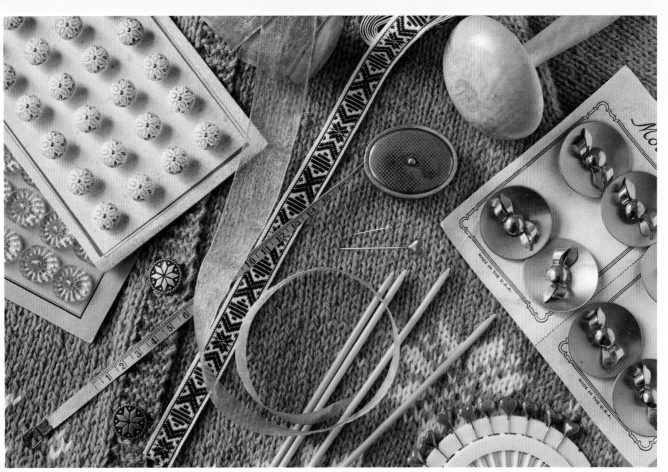

INDEX